MW01641232

All That Bright Light

A Soul Uncovered

The story of an idealistic young girl who dreamed of helping the wounded warriors and instead died at the hands of the man she tried to save. Her shattered family struggles to survive the grief and loss and ultimately find healing in the transforming power of love.

Alice G. Miller, PhD

ISBN: 9781493581665
ISBN: 149358166X

Contents

one

Losing Lulu

"Love knows not its own depth until the hour of separation"

–Kahlil Gibran

Like so many tragedies, the one in our family unfolded with no warning. Of course there were warnings, but you would have to have been paranoid or highly attuned to evil to recognize them. We did not. What happy family ever imagines that their beloved child will meet a tragic death?

Not so long ago, I held that child, my bright, beautiful granddaughter, and I fell in love that first moment I held her infant body in my arms. The world knew her as "Michelle." But, Stan, my husband, and I called her "Lulu" almost from the day she first toddled and shot us her mischievous grin. It was that wonderful little smile that lit up her face, and usually signaled that, once again, our bright little imp was up to something. And for the next 17 years Lulu continued to light up our lives.

Michelle lived her brief 17 years to the fullest. In her younger days she was our "Little Lulu," who sat in the garden and shared tea with a raggedy teddy bear family. But, growing up with her brother Patrick, her cousin, Brian and a host of neighborhood boys, Michelle quickly dropped the "little" part of her nickname and became the feisty, little girl who believed that anything a boy could do, she could do better, if she just tried hard enough. Soon, she was calling herself "Army Girl" and whenever possible, dressing in camouflage.

So, it was not too surprising that when it was time for Michelle to attend a birthday party for her older brother, Patrick, she was highly indignant when she realized that she was to be wearing a little pink dress covered in ruffles. Because she knew that she would not be winning this argument with her mother, Michelle just moved into her contingency plan and topped the outfit with her brother's heavy duty football helmet, which she wore for the remainder of the party.

"That's not in my game plan," became Michelle's response to any suggestion that some dreams just won't fly. So, this was our "Lulu" the precious little girl, who at age nine, believing that nothing was impossible, shared her latest goals with me.

"Allie," I'm planning to be a famous movie star," she informed me. "But," she added solemnly, "if it looks like that won't work out, then my back-up plan is to become a neurosurgeon." And that was our little "be all you can be" girl.

By the age of 17, the "Lulu" title was history. (Although Santa still kept sending presents for "Lulu." Because Santa knows.) Michelle had now morphed into an honors student, athletic star, tutor and friend to so many. Wild and free, she was filled with life and spirit. Her teammates recognized this and called her fearless.

So it was no surprise that when an aggressive Army recruiting team came to her high school last October, Michelle harkened back to her early childhood "Army Girl" dream. She heard only the recruiter's siren song of "be all you can be."

The Army recruiters convinced Michelle to sign up with the promise of a college scholarship and ROTC membership en route to becoming an officer and a psychologist. In the remaining months of her senior year, Michelle poured heart and soul into the new recruit training sessions, which she viewed as the road to fulfilling a new dream; working with the returning military "wounded warriors."

"Allie, I'm just so happy," she confided, soon after signing up. " I have found a new direction for my life."

By April she was dead.

Now Michelle's bright light is gone from this world. Although there has been extensive media coverage of the tragic death of a 17-year old army recruit, who died at the hands of the sergeant who was her supervisor, there has been no one who could ever put the pieces together.

Newspaper and television reporters have told and retold the story of the brave young girl who responded to a suicide call and raced off into the night to save a fellow soldier. Sadly, the sergeant, who made that call, used two bullets that night. Only one was for himself, the other bullet ended in the brain of the trusting girl who came to save him.

This country has been numbed by the countless stories of youth who have lost their lives at the hands of violent predators. We should not ever forget that these young lives will never be "yesterday's news" for the survivors. For them, the circle of grief never ends.

It seems like every day the media reports another story of one more child lost to a violent death. The news moves on, but the scars remain. Murder is never just one death, the pain ripples through a family and a community.

All too well, I know this to be true. As a psychotherapist I have walked with many families as they have struggled with loss and grief. Now I know that pain firsthand, for our beloved Lulu now lies in the ground; her grave a silent testimony to the loss that has shattered all those who loved her.

I cannot begin to understand, let alone condone, what twisted thinking precipitated the sergeant's vicious behavior. I can only speak out with a first- person account of what this tragic death has meant to a family and a community.

We never saw it coming. Like many happy families, we thought we had forever. But, on that fateful April night when the shots heard around the country were fired, we lost our beloved "Lulu" forever. As grandparents, for Stan and me, the loss is so painful that we can barely contain our grief.

My heart goes out to her parents, Kevin and Pacita and her brother, Patrick, whose pain and loss is so greatly multiplied. This family of four, now a family of three, must live each day with the grief that Saint Paul would call "the sighs too deep for words."

We had always known that as a family we were so fortunate. It was just so easy to take that good fortune for granted. Our children had married happily and given us three wonderful grandchildren

When our son, Kevin, brought Pacita home as his bride we knew that we had been truly blessed. So, Patrick, their first born arrived into a house of love. For five years he reigned as the little prince – adored by all. The little prince was ecstatic when he was told that a new baby was on the way. When he was shown the first sonogram pictures, Patrick became even more excited.

"Oh-h," he squealed in delight. "It's a puppy!"

The puppy turned out to be Michelle. Stan and I as grandparents had the pleasure of bringing one excited little boy to the hospital to meet his new little sister. The visit was sheer joy until departure time arrived. Then the little prince suddenly realized that the tiny bundle that was his sister would be remaining in her mother's arms, while he would be leaving with his grandparents, who by now had become, most definitely, second string.

As we exited down the hall, leading our sobbing little boy, a sweet grandmotherly woman came over to express her condolences for what must have been a tragic family loss.

"It's okay," I reassured her. "We just became a big brother." She nodded with the knowing smile of one who has been there.

But, happily, when mother and baby returned home the next day it was Patrick who greeted his baby sister with open arms and insisted on holding her. And for the next 17 years Patrick's arms were always open for his little sister. The family had gained a little princess. But, he would always be the little prince. And that's the way it was.

Those two children grew up as the center of their parent's world. Now, in retrospect, I can only say, "Thank God they knew that." After Michelle's death I mentioned to Pacita how glad I was that during Michelle's short life her mother had always spoiled her.

"Mom," chided Pacita, "You spoiled her, too."

"Yeah," I admitted. "And I'm glad..."

"And," added Pacita, "so did Tara."

And so she did. Tara, my daughter, loved introducing her niece to the world of consumerism. No shopping trip with her little neophyte mall rat ended without Michelle clutching a little bag containing the latest bauble her aunt had decided would look just right on Michelle.

As "Lulu" morphed into "Michelle" her creativity and humor blossomed. She often disappeared into my den and left little notes hidden among my papers.

Sometimes, I discovered them weeks later. One, from an early Christmas Eve, I found years later:

"MERRY CHRISTMAS EVERYBODY

Ho		
	Ho	
		Ho

Allie loves her grandkids especially the girl"

She loved presenting the gift of a little poem if the recipient had pleased her. My favorite is written in the slanting lines and scraggly handwriting of a young child. Now, matted and framed, the poem still hangs in my office.

"Alie, from when I was a BaBy you loved me so much, I Love you to Because of how you Love and Other things to."

As she grew older, Michelle became interested in my current writing projects. Recently, I have been writing about becoming a psychotherapist and working with adolescents over the years. Michelle always put aside her texting to peruse my latest chapter.

"That's really good, Allie," she would nod approvingly. I loved those times.

When Patrick and Brian turned 18 and graduated from high school, Michelle labored over the production of beautiful scrapbooks for each boy. With photos and comments she lovingly documented their lives. We both knew that neither of the boys would be making a scrapbook when Michelle turned 18.

"It's just not a guy thing," she shrugged.

"When you're 18, we'll write your scrapbook together," I promised her. Now Michelle's 18th birthday is approaching and there will be no shared book. Instead, she lies in the cemetery at Saint Mary's, her grave covered with notes and flowers; a silent reminder that indeed, guns do kill people. As her family we return to stand over that grave to talk to our beautiful girl and to shed a few tears.

Sometimes I just stare at that dark mound of earth and see that stubborn, fearless, little girl going out bravely into the dark, never doubting that she could save that disturbed man.

"Oh Lulu, I wanted so much to write our book together," I cry. "Now it's just me and I can only tell my story. And it's about losing you."

So, Lulu, this book's for you, baby.

I can almost hear you saying, "That's really good, Allie."

two

The Longest Night

By the time we realized the unfolding tragedy in our family it was much too late. Instead, our lives just unraveled. I can still remember, as if it were happening now:

It is the day before the last day of our granddaughter Michelle's short life. Just another pleasant Saturday in the life of a busy high school senior. Many happy hours are being spent with her mother, Pacita, picking out just the right gown for the upcoming senior prom. It is to be their last special time together. Tomorrow has already been reserved for an afternoon with a best friend. This is going to be another one of those delightful, spontaneous, idle times that are the luxury of soon- to-be high school graduates.

Sunday dawns bright and clear and the girls gleefully head off in Michelle's almost new Honda CRV. Actually, it is her mother's CRV, but it has now become Michelle's car. Her mother is driving the old Toyota, because she is so sure that the newer car will ensure Michelle's safety. But, as it turns out, all the mother love in the world will not be able to keep her daughter safe.

On this beautiful afternoon the girls spend their hours tootling around nearby Lake Needwood. It will be weeks later that Michelle's parents will view the cell phone recordings of those two happy young girls aimlessly driving through the countryside.

Now, forever history, only the images remain: two free spirits, alternately laughing and then belting out the lyrics of a current song. The off-key singing is clearly far less important than the intense volume and the joyous laughter of two girls who, for the moment, have not a care in the world.

Neither girl realizes that in a few hours Michelle's life will be over.

When Michelle returns home, tired and happy, on this clear April night there is no hint of what is about to happen. As usual, she quickly heads upstairs to wash that long, shiny hair of which she is so proud.

Like many teenage girls, Michelle has not limited herself to one hair color. Her own beautiful, rich brown hair has recently been rendered into a bright golden blonde. It is now gradually returning to its original color, slowly morphing into a fall of soft, golden brown sprinkled with highlights.

The fateful night of April 7 has now begun. It starts as a typical family Sunday night: computers, shared television, cell phones and texting are all simultaneously in progress. Michelle, her hair still damp, now dressed in an old shirt, sweatpants and flip flops, sprawls on the couch, her long legs dangling over the side.

Pacita, the industrious member of the family, sits to one side, clipping the shaggy coat of Chloe, the family dog, a fluffy little bundle of yips and wet kisses.

It is a little after 8:30 now and Michelle has just gotten a text. And with that call, life as they have known it, is about to be over.

"I've got to go right now," announces Michelle. "One of my platoon members is feeling suicidal and I've got to help him!"

"That doesn't sound like a very safe thing to do," responds Kevin. "I'll go with you."

"No, Dad, I know this guy and he's harmless," Michelle answers. She explains that this is just a young, mixed-up kid and that she can reassure him. And that is the start of the little lie that will cost Michelle her life. She knows full well who this man is and that he is not another teen-age recruit in the program. She also knows that if her parents realize this she will not be allowed to leave the house.

Michelle, a master at bargaining, has finally bartered an agreement with her parents. She can leave now but, upon arrival she will immediately text her address and she will definitely be home by 10 p.m.

"I'll text you," are Michelle's final words to her parents. They wave goodbye, unaware that this is to be the last time that they will see their daughter alive.

Ten o'clock comes and goes. But the promised text has never arrived. By midnight Kevin and Pacita are now becoming uneasy and began to call all of Michelle's friends.

"Where could she be?" they ask. "Does anyone know who this young friend is?" only then, to their dismay, her parents discover that the "young friend" is actually the 31-year old sergeant, who is her Army reserve recruiter, and lives "somewhere" in the neighboring suburb of Germantown.

All too soon, they learn that Michelle has supposedly texted a close friend to tell her that she loves her and then the text abruptly ends. Immediately, there is a new text containing only the word "goodbye." The wording does not read like Michelle's speech pattern. Her parents are now alarmed and call the police.

When the police arrive to take a report they are quick to reassure the family that in most of these "cases" the teen has just decided to stay out late and returns home unharmed. They try to locate an address for the sergeant but, even the police are unable to locate him as he apparently has moved recently, leaving no forwarding address.

In the early morning hours, Kevin is able to locate a friend who once visited the sergeant's apartment and, although she did not know the address, she is able to supply several landmarks in the area. Now desperate, Kevin and Pacita decide that Pacita will maintain a vigil by the phone at home while Kevin drives through the streets of Germantown searching for their daughter's car.

At long last Kevin spots the familiar Honda parked haphazardly in front of a darkened apartment building. He knows that he has found the home of her recruiting sergeant. His mind races with those few words known to every worried parent: "Let her be safe. Just let her be safe..."

Racing up to the apartment, Kevin bangs repeatedly on the front door. But, it is to no avail. Now he pounds frantically on the darkened windows, only to be met with silence.

Filled with the terror that only the parent of a child in danger can know, he makes an urgent call to the police. Waiting for their arrival is agony. He is pacing around the house now; waiting for a sound, waiting for the lights to come on, waiting for a sign of life.

Finally the police arrive. Now they, too, are worried. As the officers prepare to break in the door, Kevin is motioned to the back. He will not be allowed to enter. So he can only wait alone in the dark as the police force their way into that too silent apartment.

"Time all ran into weirdness," Kevin later recalls, not knowing how to describe those long minutes of waiting and anguish. Each moment has stretched into an eternity as all hope begins to die.

At last two officers return through that broken door. Silently, they stand on either side of him. But he can read the words in their eyes. In the pain that passes all understanding, Kevin can hear those words before they are spoken:

"She's gone."

three

She's Gone

"Blessed are those that mourn, for they shall be comforted."

–Matthew 5:4

"She's gone."

Unless you've been there you can't really know what happens when you hear those heart-stopping words that you already realize will change your life forever. This is one of those times. Today will soon become a day of screams and sobs.

For Stan and me it is all starting early this Monday morning as Stan picks up the phone to hear the two word message: "Call me." It is in the strangely quiet and strangled voice of our son, Kevin.

"Michelle is missing," is Kevin's terse response to our return call. "I'm at the apartment where her friends think she went... ...the police are here now.....they're getting ready to break in the door... ...I'll call you back... ..."

As Stan waits for the return call, I grab my cell phone and head for the den to call my brother, Dana and sister-in-law, Mary. Together we have always been the supporters in each other's family dramas. Ellen, his daughter, visiting from New Jersey, senses the crisis and hovers by the phone. All too soon we are interrupted by Stan, who has entered the den suddenly looking gaunt and grim-faced.

"She's gone."

The background screaming is so loud that I cannot even hear the remainder of Stan's words as he recounts Kevin's message that the police have now broken into the apartment and discovered that Michelle and the sergeant that she went to rescue are both dead

I am beginning to go numb. It feels like I am just an observer watching from afar. This cannot be real. Inside though, I know that it is real. The little girl that I have loved is now gone forever. All that terrible screaming, I realize, has been coming from me.

"We're on our way," says Dana, ending the call and postponing whatever other plans they might have had.

For Stan there is another painful call to be made before we can race over to be with Pacita. Patrick must be notified so the family can be together before the police and the crisis team arrive. Pacita must not be left alone to hear the news that will destroy her life.

"You're lying!" screams Patrick when he receives the call. "No....not Michelle..."Surely this is not true. Standing beside Patrick is Jima, the girl he will one day marry, who is already a part of the family. She has just grasped the reason for Patrick's screams.

"No!" Now the screaming is coming from Jima. She has lost, not just a dear friend, but the girl she calls her little sister.

Tara, our daughter, has already been called at work. She is so shaken that a good friend has volunteered to leave work and drive her to the house. There she will be met by her husband, John, with another shoulder to lean on.

It is only minutes before Dana and Ellen arrive at the door. I can only guess how fast they must have driven. Ellen enfolds me in her arms as I sob for the little girl, who was my baby, too.

Poised to tear out the door, I am suddenly brought to my first rational thought of the morning. Staring into my face are the soulful, questioning eyes of our other "Lulu." This beautiful young Doberman who we adopted only a few weeks ago was named after Michelle, because they both shared the same impish free spirit. Our Michelle as a dog lover was thrilled to have a namesake that she could hug and fuss over.

Now I cannot leave Lulu locked up alone in the house for what may be a very long time. I do not have dog lover friends with fenced yards. In desperation I call Dr. Popa, Lulu's caring and compassionate vet. Within minutes his assistant arrives to greet Lulu who happily trots after her and hops into the van for a trip to see her favorite vet. Now we can tear off to reach Pacita.

Fortunately, Stan has arrived ahead of us. He finds Pacita pacing with anxiety.

She is joined by her friend, Cathy, the mother of one of Michelle's best friends. During the early morning Cathy has been informed by her daughter that Michelle has not shown up to school and that she is missing. Aware that this is every parent's nightmare, Cathy comes over and stays with Pacita while Kevin on the road looking for their daughter.

They are waiting for Kevin to call or return home. However, they do not realize that he will be unable to leave the crime scene until the police can spare a driver for they fear that he is far too shaken to drive. Kevin is afraid to deliver the news until he can be sure that Pacita is not alone.

Frantic with anxiety, Pacita recounts that Kevin has said he will be calling right back. Now Stan knows that he can no longer withhold from Pacita the news that she already suspects.

"She's gone." His words stammer in the face of such grief.

"No! No! No!" screams Pacita, throwing herself to the floor. She is like the Biblical Rachel weeping for her children after the slaughter of the innocents in the book of Jeremiah. She is the mother who refuses to be comforted for the loss of her children because they are no more.

Ellen, Dana and I arrive to a tsunami of grief. Pacita's wail is not a sound that I will ever forget. Like Rachel in the Old Testament, Pacita's own innocent has been slaughtered.

I hug Pacita. "It's going to be all right," I start to comfort her. But the words will not come for we both know that it will never be all right.

Now Kevin arrives home escorted by two soldiers who flank him for support. I don't know where they came from and I am too distracted to ask. Kevin is shaken and silent. He does not want to be hugged, needing instead to control his feelings.

Going straight for his wife, Kevin's shoulders tighten with tension. Pacita is still recovering from major brain surgery and he needs to be strong for her. Struggling to contain his own grief, Kevin reaches to comfort Pacita in hers.

With her sorrow too deep for words, Pacita also needs the comfort and spiritual support of her church. As a Presbyterian, it is my pastor, Roy, who is always there in time of need with whom I will need to talk. But Pacita is a life-long Catholic and it is a priest that she needs. So I call the administrator at St. Mary's Church and explain that we need a priest right away to help us with this tragedy.

"The priests have very busy schedules," the administrator explains. "I just can't send someone out on such short notice," she adds.

"Sorry I couldn't have planned this murder in advance," I mumble to myself as she continues to protest.

"This little girl was raised at St. Mary's," I fume. "She went to school at St. Mary's and she will be buried at St. Mary's." Now I am starting to snarl, venting my rage on the poor administrator who is just trying to do her job.

"We need a priest NOW....so get him here NOW!" I yell before hanging up.

I am not especially proud of my behavior. But after being out-of-control all morning, it feels really good to snarl.

Within 20 minutes Monsignor Amey arrives and he is the oil on troubled waters. Either the Monsignor was not told of my bad behavior or he has already forgiven me for he is very warm and kind. Already I find him to be a comforting presence. Here is a priest who can be the connection with God that Pacita so desperately craves.

As the day wears on, Mary and Ellen bring in food and drinks to share. People who did not even realize that they were hungry are now beginning to eat. Some appear to be eating just to fill the empty space inside. Others find that their stomachs just cannot deal with emotions and food at the same time.

Ellen, Dana and Mary have become part of that quiet, caring presence that helps to provide a haven for people whose grief cannot be healed with mere words. My niece, Karen, has been called and already had dropped everything to schedule a flight from Boston. She will arrive tomorrow with Michelle's cousin, Olivia.

As a Filipina, Pacita has strong ties to a large community of caring. Word-of-mouth has spread rapidly for Pacita is one of their own. More people begin to drift in and we are surrounded by tears and love and food. Whenever Filipinos gather there will always be mountains of food, for food is love and food is nurture. The Filipinos have always known this.

People seem to be floating aimlessly in all directions. The few smokers gravitate to the patio. Patrick wanders aimlessly through the house looking like a lost soul. Thankfully he is joined by Jima. She has been his partner and soul mate for so long that it seems as if she has always been family.

Jima mourns the loss of her little sister. Michelle went everywhere with her; shopped with her, traded clothes with her and occasionally squabbled with her. And they both always knew that one day Michelle would be Jima's maid of honor. The loss brings tears to Jima's eyes. But Patrick, more like his father and grandfather, is still silent and numb with his own sorrow.

With the departure of the Monsignor the police arrive in the person of homicide Detective McNerney. Immediately the detective closets the family for a private session in the den.

"You are not going to like what you hear," the detective warns us. He was right, we don't. "It was a murder-suicide," he states, not attempting to varnish the truth.

We are told that at the front door of the sergeant's apartment the police have discovered an assault rifle with multiple rounds of ammunition. There appears to be no explanation for this. Or, at any rate, none is forthcoming. Still, we continue to press for the details that we fear hearing. Ultimately though, we all feel that knowing is better than not knowing.

"The two were sitting in the shower," continues the detective. "Michelle appears to be kissing the sergeant on the cheek or whispering in his ear. The sergeant shot her through the left temple, then killed himself."

Everyone is silent for a moment. We are envisioning our brave, naïve, little Michelle, still thinking that she could save him – right up until the bullet entered her unsuspecting brain.

The detective shares our outrage at the callous selfishness of suicidal people who seem to assume that they have the right to take an innocent life with them. How, I wonder, do the police, who must regularly deal with repeated horrors and tragedies, handle dealing with all the ongoing traumas? Surely, they must need to step away and just forget for awhile. Michelle, for them, must have to be just one more case.

"Will other cases come along and push her off the radar," I wonder aloud.

"I speak for the victims," answers Detective McNerney. He assures us that the police will stay with this case however long it takes.

He has been very kind, even to the point of providing his own cell phone number in the event that we should need to contact him.

After learning the details of her daughter's death, Pacita is now on information overload and needs to return to her supporters. Between hugs and tears she continues to call her family in the Philippines and friends near and far.

Already, the people who are not yet here are starting to make travel plans. Vangie, her sister, is preparing to leave from Spain so that she can be at Pacita's side as soon as possible. The kindness of family and friends is overwhelming.

As the afternoon winds down, the house is filled with Michelle's friends who have been told about her murder by their teachers after the last class period. There are more tears and mementos as the girls fill the mantle area in the front room with flowers and Michelle's lacrosse equipment. Soon photographs and trinkets are added to what is now rapidly becoming a shrine.

Pacita still cannot eat. Instead she wanders among her friends and family, stopping for hugs and tears. At times she appears to be so numb and exhausted that we all fear that she will drop.

Kevin's pain is palpable. Mostly he is silent. Like a rock, he continues to pour his own grief into a concentrated effort to ease Pacita's. I suspect that he thinks that he must appear to be far stronger than he actually feels. He has already lost one precious girl. He will not risk losing another. His tears will come later.

It is close to midnight now and time for Stan and me to go home so we can return early tomorrow. I hug Pacita, who now sits quietly. She barely seems to recognize us. For now, Pacita has been granted the temporary calm of the numbness that often follows the shock and pain of grief too deep to bear.

Kevin, who has been the solid rock of support all day, is now alone in the den staring at his computer. A casual observer might assume that Kevin is escaping into the mindless relief of the cyber world. But it is not the random world of the net that has his attention.

Kevin, the stoic, is slowly trolling through a series of photographs of his beloved daughter as the tears, now unchecked, slide silently down his cheeks.

four

Night Of The Balloons

"Grief shared is half grief, joy shared is double joy."

–Honduran proverb

Tonight is the unforgettable night of the balloons. It was on Monday, only yesterday that Michelle's death became real. Yet, here we are on Tuesday night clutching helium balloons and wandering through the crowded stadium at Rockville High School. Friends, teammates, parents and teachers have come from miles around to honor the life of our Michelle, even as they mourn her death.

I am still amazed by the speed with which this event has materialized. It has been little more than 24 hours since Michelle's closest friends have received the staggering news that she has died a terrible death.

In the throes of their grief, her friends have felt charged to take some action.....to make something happen. So almost instantly they have: arranged a balloon vigil; obtained permission to open the high school's huge stadium; borrowed a sound system and scrounged up hundreds of helium balloons.

Once again that old adage has been proven to be right: If you have an impossible task to accomplish, give it to a young person. They will not know that it is impossible and will get it done.

As I watch hundreds of people stream through the high school parking lot I give thanks for the ease of today's digital world. Technology has allowed a few girls to mobilize an entire community to come and honor one of their own who is now gone.

Everyone has been notified to bring balloons inscribed with their own loving goodbyes. The girls, who have thought of everything, have managed to locate a donor who has provided extra helium balloons to assure that everyone will have the opportunity to fly their own final heartfelt goodbye.

There are hugs and tears as we work our way through the crowded parking lot and into the stadium. Jammed together like this, it seems that everyone realizes that sometimes being sad together is easier than being sad alone. The kids are huddling in forlorn little groups, still wondering and asking: "Why? How could this happen?"

Inside, the stadium throbs with loud music that only someone under 25could love. Clearly, this is a very adequate sound system for it pulses with a CD of Michelle's favorite songs played at full volume. This is just as it should be. Michelle would have loved it.

I am touched by the kindness of people who keep stopping to tell us all about Michelle's many attributes. Her contagious excitement and joy of life, they remind us, meant that it was always fun to be around Michelle. Everyone commented on her academic honors and her athletic prowess as a star in soccer, basketball and lacrosse. Of course, we already knew all these things but never tired of hearing them again.

Repeatedly, I am reminded that Michelle, the athlete, was fearless. This I know to be true. She was fearless throughout her life. If a physical challenge seemed too difficult she just tried harder. "Suck it up and do it" was her motto. And all too frequently this was also the unsolicited advice that she passed on to family members when she felt that they could use a little motivation.

All the shared stories of Michelle's achievement fill me with pride. But what touches me the most is hearing how the younger players looked up to her and how she always had time for them. Beginner or star, to Michelle everyone was valued as an important part of the team. And this, to me, will always be what made Michelle so special.

Her classmates, too, recognize and value these same qualities. Their grief is multiplied by the knowledge of the brutality of the violent death of this friend who was loved by so many.

Tonight I hear these kids using different words to express the same painful feelings that Jackie Kennedy uttered so many years ago after another bullet entered another brain: "... ...all that bright light gone from this world."

This is not a night for a lot of speeches. It is just a spontaneous coming together. Michelle's lacrosse team appears on the field in their pink tee shirts, which are now adorned with large black letters reading: "#1 on the field#1 in our hearts."

After Michelle's closest friends share their feelings they pass the microphone to Kevin, her father. Unprepared to address the crowd, he just speaks from the heart and touches everyone:

"I can only hope that Michelle has some idea of how proud of her we were. How amazed that she was able to do so much in such a short time and most of all how much we loved her. I hope that she can see how the community has come together in grief and love for her."

Pacita, mute with the grief of a mother's loss, can only nod in agreement as the tears stream steadily down her cheeks.

As the April light dims in the sky it is now time to wind down. But we all need a fitting closure to this evening of goodbyes. And now the closure comes.

The vigil planners have been told that stray balloons can cause environmental problems as they lodge in trees and shrubs. And as a tree-hugging greenie I support this. However, a strange thing is happening. For tonight I am not the only one who is experiencing a temporary bout of amnesia.

"Release the balloons," a clear, young voice booms through the sound system.

We have been waiting for this moment. It is truly awesome as hundreds of brightly colored balloons seem to light up the sky as they float through the last rays of fading sunlight.

For a few moments the stadium is silent as we all watch our balloons, which like Michelle's bright spirit, are now heading for the heavens.

five

Sighs Too Deep For Words

"The spirit helps us in our weakness; for we do not know how to pray as we ought, but that very spirit intercedes with sighs too deep for words."
–Saint Paul's letter to the Romans

It is a place of sighs and grief at the house that so recently was home to Michelle. As the reality of her death sinks in, the reminders are everywhere. Viewing the family photographs is an exercise in pain. In some of the photos, which have been taken as recently as last week, Michelle pulls at my heart as she smiles at the camera, her face so full of life and hope.

We are numb with grief. It is the community of caring that holds us up. Every day the house is filled with family and friends. They provide the hugs and quietly go about picking up all the areas of functioning that we seem to have temporarily lost.

All week long Pacita's extended family and the community of Filipino friends have arrived in full force, bearing love, support and, of course, mountains of food. If there was actually going to be a reincarnation in this world, I would like to come back as a Filipina. They have been so filled with compassion and caring that everyone feels warmed by their presence.

Vangie, Pacita's sister, has arrived from Spain. How like Pacita she is: nurturing, caring and supportive. She is just one of those people who quietly do all the myriad of tasks that escape everyone else's attention. And always, her arms are open for her grieving sister.

At this time, as the sighs that are too deep for words paralyze the family, Karen, my niece, appears from Boston with Olivia, her daughter and Michelle's cousin. Olivia is silent and overwhelmed with the awareness of the tragedy.

Karen is caring in action. She is the one who arranges funeral programs and obituary notices. She is the one who sets up a funeral fund. At first, I cringe at the mention of donations. But it is Karen who has the sensitivity to realize that Kevin and Pacita have been plowed under with staggering medical bills. Pacita is still recovering from brain surgery after a large cyst came close to ending in tragedy.

Michelle's high school friends continue to appear with flowers, trophies and tears. The living room mantel has become a shrine to the memory of their lost friend.

"Carmen," the lacrosse stick, with which Michelle has already racked up two goals this season, is propped against the wall. Later "Carmen" will return with the team. She is going to be shared by teammates as they pickup future victories in the name and spirit of Michelle.

It has often been said that you can tell a lot about a person by observing what sort of friends they pick. That being the case, I am very proud of our Michelle. We are all impressed by the kindness of her friends and they continue to be a source of support for the family.

Even in their own mourning, the teens priority in this tragedy has been to bring action to their grief. The day of Michelle's death the boys and girls lacrosse teams were to have had their big games with Magruder High School.

When Michelle's death was announced, the games were postponed and instead the players went to their high school where they spent the better part of the evening decorating pink and yellow t-shirts to honor Michelle, who always wore jersey number one. The newly decorated shirts read in bold letters: "#1 ON THE FIELD - #1 IN OUR HEARTS."

Now, more t-shirts are being printed with Michelle's photograph emblazoned on the front and "ANGEL WATCHING OVER US" on the back. The shirts will be sold as support for the funeral.

Already the Rockville High School Student Government Association has produced and distributed camouflage bracelets reading, "Michelle Strong. Army Strong....In loving memory of Michelle Miller." I am not usually a fan of rubber jewelry but I wear my bracelet with pride.

"Just suck it up," was Michelle's favorite expression when things got tough. It was advice that she followed in her own life. But it is not advice that I am finding very useful right now.

It seems like every day brings a new awareness that Michelle is really and truly gone. Kevin and Pacita have left for the painful task that is now overdue. The viewing and the funeral are looming ahead and they must select a coffin. Yes, she is truly gone...

I remain in the house just hanging around and trying to find ways to be useful. Mostly, I answer the door to greet and comfort all those who come. Much of the time they are the ones comforting me.

Now Kevin and Pacita return. They have selected a very fine gold colored coffin. It has been a taxing afternoon and they are tired and drained. So I will continue as the keeper of the door. All too soon I am presented with the opportunity to take Michelle's advice and "just suck it up."

This time the new arrival is a tired-looking, middle-aged woman. She is here with yet another floral delivery. I smile and thank her profusely. Yet, she remains at the door and shows no sign of leaving.

I smile. The weary woman sighs. The silence stretches between us. It has been a long day and I want her to leave.

"You go now," I consider suggesting. Instead, I thank her again and begin to close the door.

"Wait," implores the woman. "Is this the house where the murdered girl lived?"

"Yes it is," I reply in a tight, firm tone that would inform most people that it was now time for them to leave.

Too late. A weary Pacita has appeared at the top of the short flight of stairs above the entryway. She is clutching a large, framed photograph of Michelle.

"Would you like to see my daughter's picture?" asks Pacita.

"Oh Yes!" The woman, now energized, enters the house and bounds up the short flight of stairs. She grabs Michelle's portrait from Pacita's hands and begins to slide her fingers across Michelle's face.

"Yes! Yes!" I am channeling her now," the delivery woman whispers. We have already had one channeler earlier this week. That was a very difficult experience for everyone. This one is just too much.

Pacita has been through enough for one day. She does not need this. By now I am considering pushing our little intruder down the stairs. But Pacita does not need that either. Besides, I really try to be non-violent.

"Mommy, mommy, I miss you..." intones our mystical visitor. "I... ..." she stops for a breath as I gently and non-violently interrupt her. Planting my hand atop hers, I firmly slide her hand to one side and replace it with mine.

"I am channeling Michelle right now," I inform the surprised woman as I slide my hand across the picture. "Michelle is telling me that she is with God now and that she is very happy." My other arm is now gently, but firmly around the channeler's shoulders.

"Thank you so much for your concern," I add as I usher her out the door. "Goodbye now."

Non-violence works.

It is amazing. Food, that gift of love, is arriving just when Pacita and Kevin need it the most. And so do I. The Rockville High School teen's parents have signed up to provide a month of dinners to the family. And here they are. Until now I was unaware that I had not eaten today. Never has food tasted so good.

The good people from the Barbeque shop, Subway and the Italian restaurant have all gifted us with food that is consumed during the day as people continue to drop by.

I just want to tell all those good people, "Thank you. Thank you. Thank you." In times of tragedy we tend to forget little things like sleeping and eating. But when someone arrives with the nurture of food and caring it feeds both body and soul.

The evening meal is over and several of us gravitate out to the patio. The night air is calm and for a few minutes I quietly sip my coffee and relax, as if this was just another night.

How touching, I think, that Pacita with all her troubles has taken the time to set out a bowl of crunchy snacks for us to enjoy with our coffee. After the first few handfuls of munchies I begin to wonder if this is some kind of traditional Filipino snack that I lack the culinary sophistication to appreciate. To me, it tastes like gravel. Later, in the kitchen, I try to find a less rude way to mention this to Pacita.

"Oh, Mom," laughs Pacita, "that's the dog's food. I forgot and left it out on the table. Soon she is laughing hysterically as she recounts my goof to everyone in the kitchen.

When another friend enters the kitchen, Pacita, still laughing, reaches into the refrigerator and graciously hands her friend a small, meat hors d'oeuvre. As her friend politely nibbles at what is actually another doggie treat, everyone in the kitchen roars with laughter.

By now Pacita is laughing so hard that she rolls to the floor. Soon everyone is laughing hysterically. As others enter the kitchen to see what all the commotion is about, the incident, which actually wasn't that funny, is told and re-told. Each time it becomes funnier as the hysteria builds.

It is the first time in days that there has been laughter in this house. No one wants it to stop. That laughter feels so good. And sometimes in life a touch of hysteria is just what you need.

As evening falls it is time for the novenas. In the Filipino tradition the grieving community gathers together for nine days. Each evening the mourners join in prayers, saying the rosary and singing hymns. It is an experience that speaks of deep spirituality and is both mesmerizing and calming.

"Are you a smoker or an atheist?" one community member asks when he spots a woman ambling out to the patio just as the novenas are beginning. Actually, neither category is accurate. She just has her own private way of dealing with sorrow.

I too, miss the novenas but for a different reason. My tears pour out every time the group sings. Instead, I sit in the kitchen and listen to the beautiful strains of "Amazing Grace" and "Holy Holy Holy" sung a cappella by a roomful of believers.

In this context, the hymns are so mournful, yet peaceful, that I know that I will not control my tears. Music does that to me. It is both painful and healing. At home tonight I will bring out my cello and play those same songs. They are now my grief songs. Playing them I can just let go while my cello wraps its musical arms around me.

It is getting late and by now I am so tired. I just cannot hang on any longer. It is time for me to go home. I will be back in the morning. But first I need to go into my garden where there are trees and light and peace.

I will sit in the corner garden that Stan and I are setting aside to honor Michelle. There is an old stone bench there waiting for me. From where I sit I can see the beat-up old bird bath that the robins love. It is now to be Michelle's bird bath.

Perhaps my favorite robin will return. He loves to perch on the flat rock in his bath and then flutter into the water, thoroughly dousing himself. Then he hops back to his rock, shuddering in ecstasy.

Soon my robin will be joined by another robin, who is making it very clear that Mr. Robin has taken quite long enough. As I sit engrossed in their side show I will know a little peace for now.

I still cry at the drop of a hat. But being "brave" is so overrated. And I remind myself that tomorrow may be better.

Emily Dickinson would understand:

"Hope is the thing with feathers
that perches in the soul
And sings the tune without the words
And never stops at all."

six

Dress Blues

"You don't have a soul,

You are a soul.

You have a body.

–C. S. Lewis

Today we are going to say goodbye to Michelle's body. The viewing will be held from 5 to 9 p.m. at St. Mary's Catholic Church. I am not ready. I will never be ready.

Although wearing black clothing is frequently seen as a sign of respect for the deceased, our family has all decided to wear black and white. The black acknowledges her death. The white represents her youth and vibrant life.

Michelle's coffin is gold. Pacita would accept nothing less for her baby. To her, the fact that Michelle's favorite color was yellow only made the decision that much easier.

Michelle's aunts, Tara and Karen, have spent the entire afternoon dragging a carload of artifacts to the sanctuary at St. Mary's. Together, they have transformed the area surrounding the communion rail into a memory wall of Michelle's full life.

Photographs, hockey sticks, athletic equipment, poems and personal memorabilia all vie for space with camouflage uniforms and accessories. Front and center is Michelle's serious Army girl portrait. In the frame on the other side, a bright-eyed Michelle smiles at the camera. She is all decked out in the white graduation cap and gown that she will never wear again.

Patrick and Jima have prepared a continuous slide show of pictures and videos that seem to bring Michelle and all her enthusiasm into the room with us. Only once does the Monsignor need to intervene and gently point out that the contemporary music which accompanies the video is, not only a bit too loud, but also not appropriate for a sanctuary.

With the assemblage of those many symbols of Michelle's happy life, it escapes no one that within the sanctuary a cruel contrast has now emerged. The images of the vibrant girl on the screen only serve to remind us that her soul has fled that lifeless form that now lies so still in her golden coffin.

The preparations are over now and it is almost time for the viewing to begin. The immediate family has been escorted into the sanctuary in advance for a last private goodbye.

"I can't do this," I cringe as the coffin arrives and is slowly wheeled down the center aisle. No one should ever have to see a beloved child lying in a coffin. But that is exactly what is going to happen.

The coffin has now been opened. The shroud, a white cloth that covers the body, is now gently lifted from Michelle's face and folded back down her body. Later, at the funeral a pall will be placed over the coffin as a sign of Christian dignity.

We step aside so that Kevin and Pacita can be the first to see their baby this one last time. Pacita looks at her sleeping princess from whom all life has fled. Weeping, she lays her head on that still chest. Kevin stands beside her, his face a rigid mass of pain as he touches his daughter's lifeless body.

Now it is my turn to stand at the coffin. It has been too much. This is all a huge mistake. This motionless figure dressed in a dark blue uniform is an imposter. Her face is puffy and still. Her hands with their stubby, little nails are so cold. This is not my Michelle lying in the shiny gold coffin.

Except that it is Michelle, minus all life and spirit. She is immaculately clad in the Army dress blues that she had once so coveted. But the dress blues were not to be hers in her lifetime. Somehow though, Pacita has managed to secure those dress blues for Michelle in her death. I rather doubt that they were authorized. But that would not have been a deterrent for Pacita. She knows that Michelle has earned them.

"Mom," her hands are so cold," says Pacita. She needs to keep touching her little girl once more. It is as if by sheer love she can bring her back to life. It is painfully obvious that this is never going to happen.

Michelle's once finely sculpted face is now slightly pudgy and completely devoid of expression. Her beautiful blondish-brown hair is nowhere in sight. Instead, a thin braid of artificial reddish hair is tightly wound around her head.

I hover over Pacita, fearing that in stroking her daughter's head she will dislodge the braid which is barely covering the bullet wounds. I do not want Pacita to make that discovery and suffer any more emotional pain. But Pacita already knows. However much she does not want to know, she knows.

"You always tell me to 'suck it up,' honey," she strokes the still body of her daughter. "I am sucking it up, but it doesn't help."

The only comfort in this painful evening has been the steady, almost unending stream of people who keep pouring into the church. The undertaker says that after the first 1000 people they have run out of guest books. And still the people keep coming.

We are awed by the outpouring of love and respect for one young girl. I lack the words to describe the power and caring that warms me as friends, old and new, appear bringing hugs and comfort.

As the evening wears on and the line to the coffin slowly edges forward, I see face after face of the people of Saint

Mark Presbyterian, my church. Stan and I have not always been the most involved members. But that does not matter. They are here. I am feeling embraced and I cannot hold back my tears. These are our people and they are here for us.

Now, as the last viewers are departing, we know that the end has arrived. Only a few hours earlier I had dreaded the entry of Michelle's coffin with its sad burden. Now I am dreading the finality symbolized by the exit of her coffin. Is there to be no end to the ends? It is like losing her and losing her over and over again. And yet, we need these rituals.

Tonight will have been the last time on earth that we will ever see Michelle's dear face. To us, that face is still beautiful even after all the internal damage that it has suffered.

We kiss our final goodbyes and watch silently as the shroud is placed over our beloved who has already left us. Only a light click announces that the coffin lid is now closed and will remain so forever. Slowly, the golden coffin rolls down the aisle and into the night.

It is over

seven

On Eagle's Wings

"And he will raise you up on eagle's wings,
Bear you on the breath of dawn,
Make you to shine like the sun,
And hold you in the palm of his hand."
–Michael Joncas

Today we will bury our beautiful granddaughter. This is just not right. When the time comes (much later I hope) it should be our granddaughter who is burying us.

To lose a child is to lose the future. There is a time for every season. The young should grow up in the secure arms of parents and family. When the time comes, the young should then parent their own children. The parents and the older generation should have the chance to open their arms to the next generation–the future. The premature end of this dream is brutal.

Instead of being in the rhythm of the time for every season, here we are at 10 in the morning at St. Mary's Catholic Church awaiting the Mass of Christian Burial. Over 1000 people have already entered the sanctuary. The pews are filled and the standing room is jammed.

Throughout the crowd I spot the Army uniforms of the officers and enlisted men and women of Michelle's reserve unit. Their presence is a statement that Michelle, although still so young and so new, was one of their own.

"Don't count on the Army. It is the church that will comfort you through this loss," a veteran friend has reminded me. Indeed, the church is a great comfort. But the presence of these soldiers today and those soldiers with tears in their eyes at last night's viewing, tells me they too, have deep feelings for the loss of a comrade.

The gold coffin that was closed forever at last night's viewing is now entering the sanctuary. It is being borne by several young men, each a good friend of Michelle's. They have all vied to be the ones picked to share the honor of being a pall bearer for a girl so close to their hearts.

A pall is being placed over the coffin as it enters the church. Traditionally, the pall is a symbolic reminder of the baptism robe that the deceased once wore. It now reminds us that all are equal in the eyes of God.

When the opening chords of "Amazing Grace" boom from the organ, my eyes blur with tears. Because I know the words I can still sing along with the hymn. But once the readings begin I find myself zoning out. As the Monsignor begins his homily I am once more focused, wanting to hear what this kind man has to say.

"Michelle was a young woman who wanted to make a difference," he begins. And I smile remembering that I had recently described Michelle to the Monsignor as an angel – but an angel with attitude.

"I like that," he agreed. The Monsignor is clearly a priest who understands that the presence of some attitude in an adolescent and the presence of a soul in that same adolescent are not mutually exclusive characteristics. I suspect that the Monsignor remembers himself at the age of 17. He just might have had a bit of attitude himself.

Jima, who was soon to have become Michelle's sister-in-law, is still struggling to deal with the shock of Michelle's murder. She shares these feelings in the opening words of her eulogy.

"You gain strength, courage and confidence by every experience in which you really stop to look fear in the face," says Jima. "You are able to say to yourself 'I lived through this horror'" she quotes Eleanor Roosevelt. 'I can take the next thing that comes along.'"

"Michelle lived her life fearlessly, she took every opportunity to live life to the fullest," smiles Jima. "There was never a dull moment with Michelle. She would always have a smile on her face that was contagious.

She had a way about her, her presence, her attitude, her soul. She knew exactly what she wanted in life and she had a go-getter mentality and nothing was going to stop her. She lived for the moment and had fun doing so.

I will never forget the day she told me that she wanted to join the Army. I couldn't believe it, my little Michelle in this huge world fighting for our country. She had a huge smile on her face when she told me and the proud look on her face reassured me that this is what she wanted. If only she could see how beautiful she looks in her Army blues:

So honorable, so majestic, so incredibly brave.

The only thing I will ever regret is not spending more time with her. But I will cherish all the times I did spend with her and I ask you to do the same. Remember the good times you shared and keep those memories close to your heart."

When I hear Patrick deliver his eulogy I am so proud. Only a loving brother could know his sister so well and speak so fondly.

"Michelle was a soldier before she ever joined the Army. Her attitude, her mentality, her stubbornness, her will. Michelle was a soldier in life. You know, when you hear parents tell their children: 'You can do anything you set your mind to... ...'

No one ever needed to tell Michelle that. Don't get me wrong To my mom's credit she told Michelle that plenty of times but Michelle was born knowing that she was capable of anything.

She was also one of the only people I know that followed through on the whole 'When I grow up I want to be this or I want to be that' thing. For Michelle, yeah, it was the Army.

How do you describe Michelle? I could start by talking about her contagious smile...or mention her fearlessness. I could talk about her insane athleticism or that drive she had when she needed something accomplished. I could get into how caring she was for her friends, family and loved ones...or speak of how there was never a dull moment with my little sister.

But I want to start by saying this....Michelle was a soldier and I mean the definition of a soldier before she even considered joining the Army. When little girls were dressing up for Halloween as princesses or witches or some type of adorable animal, Michelle insisted on going out in full woodland camouflage, face paint and all.

When little girls were supposed to be playing with their Barbie dolls and stuffed animals, Michelle was out with my cousin, my grandfather and me playing war in the backyard.

Now don't get me wrong, Michelle had a girly side. It was probably acquired right when she started hanging out with the other girls around the ripe old age of 12, or so.

Joking aside, even though Michelle didn't get the chance to fully mature by today's standards, Michelle really did have a grasp on life that was very mature for her age. Yes, she was a teen-age girl and she definitely acted it at times but Michelle had this perspective on life that I never really understood until about her last six months in this world. She wanted to live for the moment.

I remember when she announced to the family that she wanted to join the Army. I can say with the utmost certainty that my parent's really did not favor this decision. But we talked about this...Michelle wasn't going to let a little thing like permission stop her.

So she went out and got her pamphlets, did her research and came back with some ammunition for my parents. As if persuading them wasn't enough, she also had decided that she wanted to study psychotherapy. My parent's anxiety and worst fears soon turned to pride for their daughter and the big decision she had made.

Michelle was starting to figure out this thing called life. I will never forget the first time I saw her in uniform. I was so proud of her as any big brother would be. But I also gained this new profound respect for Michelle that I can only explain as inspiration.

As I look around at all of you I am reminded just how inspirational Michelle was, not just to me but to everyone with whom she came into contact. Over the past week I have witnessed the most amazing support from countless people in this room; from people who couldn't make it today and even from people miles and miles away.

I have to thank each and every one of you because, although you may not know it, all of you have, not only helped my family to try and cope with this tragedy, but you also have helped us to remember Michelle for who she was.

I find myself asking, "Why? Why did this happen to her, to my family? to me?" But only in these last few days have I really taken a step back and realized that we aren't the only ones who have lost something....who have lost someone. I know a lot of girls and guys in this room who have lost a friend, and to some, a best friend.

I know of sports teams that have lost an amazing teammate. I know of a high school that has lost a great classmate. I know of an Army that has lost a valiant soldier. The world lost a beautiful, inspirational, fun-loving human being and I want to say that I'm sorry to all of you.

Courageous...Inspirational....Respected....Proud.... Athletic....Outgoing....Ready....Loved. These words perfectly describe what sounds like an amazing soldier to me. "Though she be little, she is fierce."

I love you, Michelle.... We love you, Michelle.

Goodbye for now but not forever."

Closing the beautiful service we all stand to sing the hymn that has graced so many funeral services: "On Eagle's Wings." The refrain continues to haunt me:

"And he will raise you up on eagle's wings,
Bear you on the breath of dawn,
Make you to shine like the sun,
And hold you in the palm of his hand."

The final moments have arrived. The local police have formed a motorcade to escort the extended family from the church to the cemetery. It is a solemn walk past the gravestones of those who went before, to the gravesite where our loved one is about to be buried.

Under a dark green awning we are all seated tightly together on folding metal chairs. My chair has one leg so deeply mired into the ground that I am actually sitting on three legs. What will happen, I wonder, if my chair falls over? These things happen to me.

I am not going to think about that. Instead, I will focus on the prayers. I try not to look at the gaping hole that will soon be Michelle's final resting place. But I must, for it is time to lay our roses on top of the coffin in our last and final goodbye.

Several officers step forward and in military precision begin the flag ceremony and rifle volley. Now the bugler steps forward to play the mournful strains of "Taps." The melancholy notes vibrate with a sadness that is touched by peace.

"Day is done, gone the sun,
From the lakes, from the hills, from the sky;
All is well, safely rest, God is nigh."

eight

A Call To Arms

"We are gathered here today to remember the life of PFC Miller. Even though she was only with the 48th a short time she touched many people's lives. Her vibrant, bubbly, go-getter attitude was an example everyone should follow. She will be missed not only by those who knew her but, by those who had just met her as well."
"Rest in Peace Sister"

–Program header for the memorial ceremony for PFC Miller.

It has been a month of long, sad goodbyes. Each, painful in its own way. Today feels like it will be the hardest. We are heading for the chapel at Fort Meade, Md., where our granddaughter, Michelle's Army Unit has scheduled a memorial service in her memory.

I do not want to be going there at all. It will just be another reminder that if Michelle, at 17, had never been recruited into the Army she would never have met the Sergeant who destroyed her life.

Instead, Michelle, at 17, bought the dream that the Army recruiter promised her. She was to complete weekend training sessions at Fort Mead during her senior year in high school. In the fall she would enter her freshman year of college with an Army scholarship. After joining the ROTC, the Reserve Officer's Training Corps, she would complete college and earn a graduate degree in psychology. Michelle would then be an officer and psychotherapist working with the wounded warriors.

All too soon that dream began to unravel. First, the Army signed up Michelle for summer boot camp. As an outstanding high school athlete, Michelle looked forward to the experience. Then she discovered that boot camp would be followed immediately by a semester of military mental health course work, in lieu of the first semester of her freshman year in college.

Weeks later, Michelle was informed that, unfortunately, the military course work session would overlap with the college's spring semester. So, by now this honors student had lost her entire upcoming freshman year in college.

So, here we are going to a military ceremony honoring Michelle. Ironically, it is just days after the family received an official notification addressed to Michelle from the U.S. Army. Adding insult to injury, the Army announced that they were now rescinding the promised college scholarship.

Michelle died never knowing that there would be no college in her foreseeable future. The high school honors courses would have been for naught. So much for the recruitment commitment. Michelle was slated to become part of the fighting force as an enlisted private.

MILLER
ARMY

I know that Michelle, our little warrior, probably would have found a way, no matter how difficult, to fulfill her deferred dreams while remaining an Army girl. So, in her memory I can do no less. Today I am going to try to view this entire experience through Michelle's eyes.

As we pull into the base at Fort Meade, we enter a sea of camouflage. Everywhere we look there are groups of young soldiers milling about. They are all sporting camo and they are all so young. These are the men and women of the 48th Combat Support Hospital Unit where Michelle was trained. They are her people.

In the chapel our family is escorted to the front row. Behind us are a couple hundred young Army recruits. They, too, are wearing the regulation camouflage. Directly facing us on the raised dais stands the grim memorial, an upended rifle. Atop the rifle is a helmet draped with a long chain which holds Michelle's last dog tags, the final reminders of a fallen soldier.

I can no longer contain my tears. I am grateful that the Army is honoring Michelle as one of their own. But, that does not slow my tears. The fallen comrade that they honor is the little girl who we so recently called our own.

In her final weeks we often referred to Michelle as our "Private Lulu." Each time she heard that affectionate title, Michelle smiled to return the affection and then immediately screwed up her face in that inimitable expression that only Michelle could master. In essence, it was a non-verbal "stick it in your ear" response.

She was the Army girl and that was that.

It was such a short time ago that I watched the video that Michelle had made of herself dressed in full camouflage. Standing erect, feet apart and hands clasped behind her back, our proud Army girl barked out the Soldier's Creed.

Soldiers Creed

I am an American soldier.

I am a warrior and a member of a team.

I serve the people of the United States, and live the Army Values.
I will always place the mission first.
I will never accept defeat.
I will never quit.
I will never leave a fallen comrade.
I am disciplined, physically and mentally tough, trained and proficient in my warrior tasks and drills.
I always maintain my arms, my equipment and myself.
I am an expert and I am a professional.
I stand ready to deploy, engage and destroy the enemies of the United States of America in close combat.
I am a guardian of freedom and the American way of life.
I am an American soldier.

Integrity-wise, Michelle lived that creed. "I will never leave a fallen comrade" was part of that credo when, as an idealistic young recruit she went out into that dark night thinking that she would save the life of a suicidal soldier. Instead she died with him.

"I will never accept defeat" was a part of that creed that Michelle had lived by long before she was recruited. I remember this and smile whenever I hold the camouflage mug that Michelle proudly presented to us after her first official visit to the base commissary. There, in large print, it reads: "There's strong and there's Army strong."

As the ceremony comes to a close, 200 young recruits stand and march to either side of the outer aisles. One by one, the recruits slowly walk forward up to the dais. For a moment, each stands at attention and sharply salutes the final memorial for the fallen comrade. Some take an extra moment to make the sign of the cross - a final goodbye to our little girl.

Looking at all these solemn young faces I pray that these recruits will remain safe and not have to face combat. But, I fear that they will not be safe. For the Middle East remains a seething cauldron where religious factions are constantly pitted against one another.

Daily these warring nations continue to demonstrate that bombs and guns have never provided a solution. It seems that the only way they will ever bury the hatchet is in each other. And I do not want to lose any more of our precious youth to this bloodshed.

Michelle heard my worries many times. But, she was 17 and such fears never seemed to resonate with her. Usually she shushed my concerns with that fearless smile.

"Allie, I want to serve my country," she always answered. On more than one occasion she clinched her reply with a reminder of the acknowledgement I had included in a book I once wrote about peace. I'm not sure that she actually read the book but, she really liked the acknowledgement:

> *"I believe deeply in peace and nonviolence but I also recognize that evil does exist in this world and that there are people who are so destructive that they must be stopped.*
>
> *Therefore, I support a military force as a defense against that evil. I can only hope and vote to create a government which will only use our military might as a defense and not as an act of aggression.*
>
> *So in this vein, I wish to gratefully acknowledge the brave men and women in the military who, over the years, have sacrificed so much to protect the freedoms that allow me to write about peace."*

As we leave the chapel one of the young Lieutenants in charge approaches me to offer his condolences and to remind me that the Sergeant "was not a representative of the Army."

"We are not like that," he continues to reassure me. Striving to express his concern, he asks "Is there anything I can do for you?"

"It would mean a lot if we could have Michelle's dog tags for the family," I suggest. "Or, could we have several," I add quickly, realizing that everyone was sure to want one.

"Wait right here," the Lieutenant promises. "I'll be right back." True to his word, he soon returns with a handful of freshly printed dog tags. Although it was not necessary, the Lieutenant once again reminds me, "We are not like that Sergeant."

I know that. I am still thinking of all those earnest young faces in the chapel. Our country should be proud of them and grateful that they are willing to be there for us.

For, like Michelle, those young recruits also have said, "I want to serve my country."

nine

Do Not Stand At My Grave And Weep

"Do not stand at my grave and weep,
I am not there, I do not sleep.
I am a thousand winds that blow,
I am the softly falling snow.
I am the gentle showers of rain,
I am the fields of ripening grain.
I am in the morning hush,
I am in the graceful rush Of beautiful birds in circling flight.
I am the star shine of the night.
I am in the flowers that bloom,
I am in a quiet room.
I am in the birds that sing,
I am in each lovely thing.
Do not stand at my grave and cry,
I am not there ---I do not die.

–Mary Elizabeth Frye

"Do not stand at my grave and weep," says the poet. But, we do stand at Michelle's grave and weep. Many times. For now the funeral rituals, ceremonies and memorials are over. The numbness is receding and we are left to deal with our new reality. Michelle is really dead. She is not coming back. We can't hug the flowers that bloom and the birds that sing. Instead, we come to the cemetery.

From the beginning, Michelle's gravesite has been banked with flowers, photos and mementos. It almost looks like a festival. With a great dose of denial that I never knew that I could possess, I sometimes fantasize that this is all unreal. At any moment Michelle, full of her usual life and spirit, is going to pop up in front of me.

"Ha! Ha! fooled you, Allie," she announces, giving me her famous, impish smile. But that hard, cold mound of raw earth tells me otherwise.

Throughout the weeks Michelle's friends and teammates continue to appear at the grave to leave their remembrances and to, yet again, say another goodbye.

They are still trying to accept the reality of those sad words that once were uttered by Jackie Kennedy after another tragic death: "... ...all that bright light gone from this world." And now when I see Michelle's friends who soon will be graduating without her, I just want to remind them to cherish and protect that bright light within themselves.

A best friend appears at the grave bearing a mass of golden tulips. Because she knows, of course, that yellow was Michelle's favorite color. Silently, her friend lays the beautiful flowers on the ground where, end-to-end they circle that sloping mound of raw earth. There they lay, mutely speaking of the grief that has no words.

The gravesite at St. Mary's is in an open woodland, quiet and still. As we sit there the occasional deer strolls through and sometimes a multitude of birds sail by, leaving a song in their wake.

Kevin and Pacita drop by every day; Kevin on his way to work and Pacita during her lunch hour. The other times they are able to come together. Stan and I join them when we can and often just slip in a visit by ourselves. They each cherish this silent time, as do we. Sometimes in life we all just need a quiet place to be.

Mother Teresa, who I frequently quote but, all too rarely emulate, has said it best:

"We need to find God, and He cannot be found in noise and restlessness. God is the friend of silence. See how nature —trees, flowers, grass—grows in silence; see the stars, the moon and the sun, how they move in silence.... We need silence to be able to touch souls."

The teen-agers continue to bring their own bright light to the grave. Often they leave small tributes: flowers; lanterns; pinwheels; miniature lacrosse sticks and balls and personal notes to Michelle.

As the notes and tributes pile up, a good friend installs a full-size mailbox clearly marked with Michelle's name. Soon another friend has left an envelope addressed only to: Michelle Miller - Heaven.

These many notes and tributes are heartfelt and private. They express deeply personal feelings and are not to be shared publically. Only recently, two friends have indicated that they would like to openly share their feelings.

One friend framed her remembrance with a question.

ROCKVILLE
1

"Who Was Michelle To Me?"

"Overall, she was a fierce, unstoppable bundle of love. As a teammate she was reliable and always an up lifter. As a classmate she was a hard worker and an encourager. And most importantly, as a friend she was loving and goofy.

She always knew the right thing to say even if it was nothing at all. I miss all of the goofy faces we made to one another. They are what got me through the school day most of the time. Michelle was a beautiful person with an even more beautiful soul. Every day, every time I pray I'll be missing her."

"Michelle," writes another friend. "It's amazing how fast time has passed but it also feels like ages since I got to see your beautiful smile or hear your one-of-a-kind laugh." Her friend shares her experiences with Michelle and adds, "We bought you some windmills and I am happy to see that you're keeping them blowing.....I also left you one of my rosary bracelets. It'll always be with you now and I'll always keep the blue version of it with me.

I'll be starting my senior year in a few weeks and I hope I can have as much fun as you did during yours. I think of you always and I hope you like it wherever you are. Keep shining and smiling. I promise we all feel it when you do."

The notes that pull the most on my heart are the ones that come from Kevin and Pacita. For, from now on, they will find themselves only writing the words that they long to be able to say to their daughter.

"Michelle, sweetie," writes Pacita.

"I am here every day, sometimes 3 or 4 times a day. I tried so many times to write down what I wanted to tell you, but instead I rather talk to you because I can tell you more than what I have to write.

I have so many things I want to tell you about how different life is now without you. Your friends are moving on to their new life. I wanted to see you so bad doing the same thing. I just wonder why things happened this way.

When I was growing up I just wanted so bad to go to college with my friends but my parents couldn't afford to send me. I dreamed to have a beautiful family and I have that (thanks to God.) All those years I have told myself that I will do everything to make sure that my family come first, before myself.

I work hard to protect you and your brother. I don't mind working two jobs so I can provide you and your brother what you need. Your father and I tried everything to make sure we are there for you and Patrick. When he was working at night, I work daytime to make sure we are there to take care of you. He doesn't mind if he doesn't have sleep as long as you are with him.

What did we do wrong, Michelle? Our dream for you to go to college (your dream rather.) What happened? You're supposed to graduate like you said to me. You said you are going to make us proud. That's why you wanted us to come and visit you.

Now what do you want us to do? I have so much to ask but I don't know where to start and I don't know who to ask these questions. I wanted to think you're at boot camp or vacation or maybe college but I am lying to myself by thinking those things.

I want you to know that life is not the same without you here with us. I also know that you are in heaven and watching all the tears that are rolling down in my face every day and night. I am sorry Michelle but I miss you so very much. I want to hug you one more time and maybe you and I have a chance to say goodbye.

Tell me, baby girl, why did it happen this way? One day you're here and one day you're gone. I don't know what did I do wrong? I love you so very much and I hope you know that much.

Bye now and I will see you later....

Love, Mom"

A small stone bench sits beneath the dogwood tree that shades Michelle's grave. It was placed there by the kind-hearted man who still remembers when Michelle and his daughter were classmates at the St. Mary's School. It is on this bench that Kevin sits alone to write yet another note to his beloved daughter.

"Michelle, I pray that you are at peace now, smiling down on us. I hope you know how much we love you and how proud we are of all that you accomplished.

Your mom is still just torn apart, I just do my best to keep it to myself. Yesterday was Father's Day and all I could think about was one more hug, or one more "I love you, Daddy" from you.

I guess I'm starting to realize I'll never see my Girlikins again. I know that I wasn't the best father, Michelle. I really tried but I'm here and you're gone.

The world has lost an exceptional girl, a caring, fearless, difference-maker. And is left with me. I let you go. I hope you know how much I love you, baby. I can only remember what was and try not to let the bitterness over what happened take over my life. "

ten

Take My Breath Away

"With every day take my breath away and make life worth everything that I've been through."

–Song lyrics quoted by Michelle Miller

It has been three months since our Michelle's death and we still wonder how this could have happened? How did Michelle's life become entwined with the disturbed man who led her to her death?

Over and over I return to those lyrics that Michelle apparently re-wrote before continually repeating them. It was almost as if they had become a theme song:

"With every day take my breath away and make life worth everything that I've been through."

The young voice that used to echo those words is now stilled forever. But, I am beginning to get a sense of the meaning that those words held for her.

Since Michelle's death I have; talked with her friends, checked the net, listened to cell phone records and read journals. The answers are there, but too late for Michelle.

On the net, the lyrics, "Take my breath away….." reappear as a theme in many songs by an assortment of writers. But, none of the songs include the line: "and make my life worth everything that I've been through." I believe that there is a reason for that. Those changed lyrics are not about Michelle.

They are about the Sergeant.

In an attempt to make any sense out of this tragedy, I have looked into the early days of this relationship and have reached my own conclusions. Only now do I realize that from that October day that Michelle first met with the Army recruiters, the Sergeant was drawn to her youth and beauty.

Clearly, from that first day, the Sergeant made a decision to pursue her, not only for the Army, but for himself. Michelle's cell phone records document that she had been receiving personal calls from him even before she had officially signed up.

Like many sexual predators, the Sergeant, while not especially attractive, was very charming and charismatic. Although it was not public knowledge at the time, the newspapers were soon to report that he was under investigation for recently having married another attractive young Army recruit. It appeared that even after that marriage he continued to have young girls in his life.

In retrospect, I wish I could have foreseen the future back in October when Michelle, laughingly informed me that her new recruiting supervisor was calling her "Baby Face."

"If one of the high school boys calls you 'Baby Face' that's cute," I warned her. "But the Sergeant is not in high school. He is 31 years old and married. He is also your supervisor." Michelle was unimpressed with my lack of coolness.

"He's hitting on you, Michelle," I insisted. "That is so NOT cute. He is way out of line. Don't get involved with him."

"Don't worry, Allie, that's not in my game plan," Michelle assured me. And it wasn't in her game plan. Not then.

Like a classic predator, the Sergeant honed in on Michelle's vulnerability. She wanted to be listened to, heard and valued as a mature young adult. It was the siren song of age 31 flattering age 17.

Michelle wanted not to be a girl but to be a woman. The Sergeant wanted not to be a man but to be a boy. At 31, he saw his youth as fleeting and so, little by little, he stole hers.

However, the Sergeant's overt message was very different. "Slow down, you crazy child," he sang, echoing the famous lyrics of Billy Joel. This became their special song. Ironically, the lyrics continue to admonish the ambitiousness of youth while pointing out that youth are also still afraid.

The Sergeant exploited that "fearful" part in every adolescent. He spoke to Michelle's uncertainties, listened to her feelings, became her mentor. She told him things "that no one else knew." And all along, he stroked, her, praised her and told her that she was more special than all other girls.

"You take my breath away...." became the theme for their relationship. Although, in the beginning it meant something quite different than it later came to mean. For several months Michelle thrilled to the experience of falling in love.

Then gradually the relationship began to shift. As the Sergeant became increasingly enamored with Michelle he also became increasingly clingy. "Every day you take my breath away." was becoming synonymous with neediness. In spite of this she still loved him and failed to grasp the implications of his actions.

"He's depressed," she told her friends when they commented on his domineering behavior. Michelle, the fiery, independent girl, tried at first to make excuses for what was happening in the relationship. The Sergeant's original delight in Michelle as a bright, free spirit was rapidly diminishing as his need to control her grew.

Overwhelmed by his needs, Michelle tried on several occasions to sever the relationship. But, each time he courted and pursued her until, once again, Michelle relented. In the records of Michelle's last days there emerges the picture of a miserable man who was now adding threats of suicide to his stance of neediness. As Michelle began to pull away he became more demanding, texting her day and night, insisting that he know where she was at all times.

It seemed as if Michelle, the bright, free butterfly that had first attracted him was now becoming objectified. For the Sergeant it was no longer enough to admire her beauty and her free flight of spirit. He had to own her, to possess her and to keep her as his butterfly specimen who could no longer fly because she was pinned so tightly to the wall.

As the suicide threats mounted, the Sergeant knew that he could count on Michelle's kind heart. She would always come to save him once again – and take his breath away. For Michelle, it must have been like trying to blow air into an empty balloon that could not expand unless she was there. Except, she was never able to fill him. If only she had told us.

With the arrival of April, Michelle's spirits began to soar. Soon it would be summer and time for boot camp, which she viewed as a new and exhilarating experience, not to mention freedom. The focus was now on her future.

Meanwhile, Michelle reveled in the excitement of preparing for the senior prom, her much awaited high school graduation and all the fun of beach week; none of which she would ever attend. For the first week in April was to be her last week on this earth.

From the existing records and words of her friends I have reconstructed what I can only presume to be her final hours:

It is a beautiful sunny, Sunday afternoon and Michelle is enjoying every minute. She is joyously driving around a local lake, laughing and singing with one of her best friends. The only dark clouds in her sky are the repeated texts from the Sergeant, angrily demanding to know why she has chosen to be with a friend rather than with him.

It will only come out much later, that the night before, when he was unable to locate Michelle, the Sergeant called another young recruit who came to his apartment to talk him out of a suicide attempt. When he finally passed out drunk, the young recruit left, assuming that the crisis was over.

Michelle remains blissfully unaware of any danger. She has chosen to remain with her friend and enjoy the freedom of their hours together. She has no way of knowing that there will be a price to pay for this.

When Michelle returns home the Sergeant's texting continues. His suicidal threats are escalating. Once again, Michelle feels that she must go to him. She has saved him before and she is quite sure that she can do it again.

So Michelle does what she had done before. She lies to her parents. She tells them that this text is from a young platoon member. She promises them that she will return soon. Perhaps she believes that this is true. But it is not true.

Michelle is completely unaware that this time when she enters the Sergeant's apartment he has no intention of allowing her to leave. Hours later the police will find her cell phone and shoes by the locked front door.

As the night wears on, the Sergeant's mood improves. Together, they walk into a late night convenience store. There a surveillance camera records the couple laughing and chatting together while he purchases a package of cigarettes.

It is only after they have returned to the apartment that everything changes. Michelle must now leave. She needs to return home for she has school classes in the rapidly approaching morning. He does not want her to leave.

Suddenly things begin to turn ugly. It has never been like this before. The Sergeant announces that it is now time. He is ready to kill himself. With a loaded gun he heads for the bathroom.

Michelle trails behind and finds him sitting in the shower stall holding the gun to his head. Not knowing what else to do, she follows him into the stall, sits on his lap and whispers the words that have always worked before. But, this time is different.

Michelle's last sensation on this earth is the cold steel of the gun muzzle pressed against her temple. Then comes the gunshot blast that, hopefully, Michelle never hears.

It has finally happened. Just like the song —he took her breath away.

eleven

To Forgive Is Divine

"To err is human,
to forgive, divine."
–Alexander Pope

Alexander Pope was right; to err is so human. And, I think, the more grievous the error the more divine the forgiveness. But I am so far from the divine and the Sergeant's error was so malignant with evil that I struggle to remain the pacifist that I want to be.

When family and friends first heard of Michelle's death several of the men vented their outrage. If only the Sergeant were still alive, they raged, then we could kill him.

"But not too rapidly," suggested one man. "Let him suffer."

The psychotherapist within me knows that the Sergeant was already suffering whether he acknowledged it, or not. At the end of his life he was depressed and suicidal.

In the early days after Michelle's death, I wanted the Sergeant to have been denied the release of his own death. Instead, I wanted him to be locked up for the rest of his life and maybe brutalized a little in the process. I am not proud of this.

I know that his suffering would not bring Michelle back. Also, what spoils the fantasy is that the actual image of anyone being tortured makes me sick to my stomach.

"'Vengeance is mine,' sayeth the Lord," is not such a bad policy to keep in mind. I have come to believe that there is no better way to corrode your own life than to be filled with bitterness and lust for revenge.

Hating on this level, suggests one Zen proverb, "is like taking poison and waiting for the other person to die." I do not plan to live with bitterness. The other alternative is to just offer it up.

This is not always so easy. I do believe that God loves us all but sometimes it is hard to understand why. God, of course, has the big picture. I just want to ask the Sergeant about the little picture.

"Why? Why? Why?" is the question that keeps running through my head. "You wanted to die." I imagine saying to him. "You wanted to die – but not alone. You called her to help you. Did you need her death to help you die?"

"By dying you never had to face a trial. You never had to listen to the survivors speak of the bright light that is now gone from this world. I wonder would that pain have touched you? If you needed to die so badly why did you not just do it to yourself?"

I believe that God may find a way to forgive the Sergeant but I will never believe that this tragedy was in God's plan. It seems that the price of free will is always going to mean that some people will use it for evil. God may intervene but I am not inclined to believe that he is always going to stop tragedies. Life has proven otherwise.

Pacita believes that while God did not stop that bullet from killing her daughter, once she had been shot, God took her home. He prevented her from remaining on this earth; brain damaged, dysfunctional and miserable. I am inclined to believe that once that bullet tore through her brain, life for Michelle was over.

I wonder where Michelle would be with the whole idea of forgiveness. As a young child she was very forgiving. Although, she usually wanted to make sure that the offender was sufficiently ostracized first.

As a preschooler Michelle attended a martial arts ceremony with the family to watch her brother perform. Since she was not featured in the program, she soon became bored and found a new toy to play with. Unfortunately, that "toy" was an expensive camera belonging to a family friend.

Several requests to return the camera fell on deaf ears as Michelle continued to tote around her new plaything. After a final warning I gently removed the camera from two unwilling little hands. "Gentle" was a relative term because Michelle had a grip like a steel vise.

I was rewarded with one of Michelle's special "If I were bigger than you, you would never have gotten this back" looks, as she stomped off to the far side of the studio where she ignored me for the next hour. Finally, I went over to join her. It was time to make peace.

"Michelle, I'm sorry you were angry," I told her, explaining why the camera was a fragile and prized possession that needed to be returned. "I didn't want to embarrass you," I added.

After a moment of thought, Michelle decided to bestow her blessing on me.

"Allie, I forgive you, she hugged me. "But I am very very dis-em-pointed in you."

I wish that it would be that easy as we get older and the dis-em-pointing behaviors in life become more serious.

"I destroy everything I care about," the Sergeant once texted Michelle. It was a message that we did not discover until after her death. Apparently, Michelle never picked up on the implications of that message.

As an idealistic 17-year old girl, Michelle lacked the experience and the judgment to recognize that this was a disturbed man. She believed that with enough love and support she could save him. So when she was texted that, once again, the Sergeant was feeling suicidal, she went off into the night to save him.

Little did Michelle know that the night before another teenage girl had received the same message. She, too, went out to save the Sergeant. Fortunately for her, he drank himself into a stupor that night. The girl then returned home, never knowing what might have happened to her or what was about to happen to Michelle.

That fateful night, when Michelle again went out to save the Sergeant, was when the evil part entered in full force. It was not enough that he was waiting with a loaded gun, ready to put a bullet into his own head. He had apparently decided that if he was not going to live this miserable life anymore, then Michelle was not going to be allowed to continue to have the happy, joyful existence that she enjoyed.

If I had known the Sergeant as a client I would have wanted to help him to understand and conquer his own demons; to build a richer life for himself. I would have worked hard to be there for him. But the bullet in my granddaughter's head changed all that.

It seems to be one of life's little ironies that the people who should feel guilty, frequently don't. And the people who need not feel guilty, frequently do.

It is, as an English clergyman stated many years ago:

"Regret for the things that we did
can be tempered by time; it is
regret for the things we did not
do that is inconsolable."

–Sydney Smith

Since the morning of Michelle's death so many good people have lamented "If only. If only…."

Some of the teenagers who were close to Michelle have wished that they had recognized the signs. Toward the end of her life, they anguished, if only they had seen it coming. But how, I ask them, could you have seen what Michelle herself did not see?

"If only I had not let her go," laments her mother.

"But," I remind her, "you didn't even know that was where she was going. So why would you have stopped her?"

"If only I had gone with her," sighs her father. I tell him how grateful I am that he did not go with her. Although no one knew it, the die was already cast. The Sergeant was going to kill himself and take Michelle with him. By the front door was an assault rifle surrounded by rounds of ammunition. Had Kevin been present he would never have left there alive. The two deaths would have become three.

The only people who could have saved Michelle were the Army people. They chose to look the other way. As time goes by more information has surfaced. Much of that information has been in the papers and is now yesterday's news.

The Sergeant was already under Army investigation and had been since last October. He had even informed Michelle that he knew this and that it was one of his concerns. The specifics of the investigation are unclear and probably always will be.

It is hard to believe that, with an investigation underway, the Army did not check out his Facebook entries. He was clearly a predator who had written sexually suggestive comments to potential recruits and posted poetry discussing suicide. It is hard to believe that this was a man the Army would select to work with young recruits.

Those who worked with him in the recruiting office must have had some concerns. But everyone remained silent while the Sergeant continued to interact with teenage girls. And that is the tragedy. Michelle's death could have been prevented if someone had had the courage to speak out.

I imagine that there are those in the Army who realize this now and suffer inwardly. Perhaps they too are saying, "If only. If only..." Our family still faces the pain of accepting this reality.

Pacita searches for healing in her own way. Although medication has been suggested to her, Pacita is adamant that medication just does not work for her.

"I just pray and pray and pray," she says. And that is what she does.

There is an old Hasidic story in Jewish lore that speaks to this. In the story a student is questioning his rabbi:

The student asks his rabbi about the wording in the Torah, which states that the Word of God is placed on our hearts. "Why," wondered the student, "does it not say 'in' our hearts?"

"Because," the rabbi answered, "people are not always able to let the Word enter into their hearts. But when God's Word is placed 'on' their hearts, it will be there when their hearts are broken open by the pains of life.

And the Word remains there ready to fall 'into' that open seam of pain.'"

And so Pacita prays.

Like Pacita, Kevin is a forgiving person. But this tragedy is not something that he can just let go of. Yet, even through this great tragedy Kevin continues to possess a generous spirit.

Never was this generosity of spirit more evident than during the period after Michelle's death when Kevin returned to the police station to pick up her car. The officer who accompanied him pointed to an older man who was just leaving the building.

"That's the Sergeant's father," the officer announced.

"At first I just wanted to deck him," remembers Kevin. But his anger was soon replaced with a deep sadness for the other man, who had also lost a child.

"It must be worse for him," says Kevin, although he cannot fathom anything worse than losing his little girl. "His son is dead too. But he died by his own hand and gun." The officer does not want Kevin to approach the man with his condolences. Kevin silently realizes how sad it is that this man is left with the added pain of knowing the destruction that will remain as his son's legacy.

I am so proud that my son's legacy is one of caring, which can bring its own peace. Martin Luther King was right. "Forgiveness is not an occasional act. It is a permanent attitude."

We all find our peace in different ways. For me, I just sit in the garden on the old prayer rock and watch as the circle of life moves on in the pond. The runty, little feeder fish that we had purchased at the price of ten per dollar grew so fat and happy that they looked like big, golden koi.

Apparently, Manny, Moe and Jack, our next generation of raccoons, also found them attractive – and delicious. In short order they have polished off every single goldfish. I might have forgiven them had they not moved on to the Blues Brothers. That frog duo used to serenade us from the flat rocks that edge the pond. Now it has been silent for weeks and weeks and the pond, though still lovely, has remained barren.

Today, as I meditate on my rock I am surprised to see that the pond water appears to be moving. Peering in, I discover that the movement is caused by hundreds of tiny swimmers. Hooray, the tadpoles are here. I have just witnessed that special moment that environmentalists experience every day: Life goes on.

I like to think of Saint Francis as the first environmentalist. His love of animals and nature set the stage for future ecologists. A man who was born to wealth and privilege, he opted instead to live humbly and spend his life in service to others. It is his prayer that has become the mantra for my own life.

The Prayer of Saint Francis

Lord,
Make me an instrument of thy peace;
Where there is hatred, let me sow love;
Where there is injury, pardon;
Where there is despair, faith;
Where there is darkness, light;
And where there is sadness, joy.
O Divine Master,
Grant that I may not so much seek
To be consoled, as to console;

To be understood, as to understand;
To be loved, as to love;
For it is in the giving that we receive,
It is in the pardoning that we are pardoned
And it is in dying that we are born
to eternal life.

–Saint Francis of Assisi

The words of Saint Francis never fail to comfort me and point out the direction for my own healing. This saint, who lived in the 13th century, is just as relevant now as he was centuries ago. His words remind me of the simple answer to my own dilemma of forgiveness.

In the words of Saint Francis:

"Our actions are our own;
their consequences belong to heaven."

It's that simple. I can just say: "God, I can forgive those who neglected to act in time. They just didn't know how high the price would be. But the Sergeant, I cannot yet forgive. I will leave him in your hands. "

twelve

For All Sad Words

"For all sad words
of tongue or pen,
the saddest are these:
'It might have been.'"
–John Greenleaf Whittier

Today is another painful reminder of what might have been – and now will never be.

It is graduation day for the Rockville High School seniors. Some of Michelle's classmates will already be trying on their caps and gowns in preparation for this evening's ceremony. But we can only look once more at the beautiful advance portrait of a smiling Michelle in the white cap and gown that she will never wear.

Time flies when you are nervous and all too soon we are at Strathmore Hall, being graciously escorted to the front row where the kindly principal has reserved seats for our family.

I will never forget the pain as we watch the robed young graduates make their solemn march to the stage where they will receive their diplomas.

Although I know better, I continue to watch in vain for the girl who will never be there. Michelle's friends are marching on without her. Instead, she remains in that last portrait, frozen forever in time.

As the last senior receives her degree there is a moment of silence. Then the principal calls out, "Michelle Lynne Miller." Kevin and Pacita are called to the stage to receive Michelle's diploma.

Pacita has been presented with Michelle's honors sash and the white mortarboard that Michelle's friends have decorated with her initials. Kevin is wearing a tasseled, woven rope that confers the additional honors that Michelle has earned.

As Pacita and Kevin exit the stage the entire hall erupts with a standing ovation that seems to thunder on forever. At least that is the way that I will always remember it.

"They are all moving on now," sighs Pacita, her eyes filled with tears. After the ceremony the students flock to the family with hugs and support. But Pacita is right. Michelle's classmates are leaving behind their high school days to enter the world of college, jobs and families. But Michelle will remain behind, all that bright light forever stilled.

The crowd is thinning now. The graduates begin to wander off together. Families group in little clusters, preparing to head off for a celebration of this happy day. Our little family cluster will be heading for the gravesite, where Michelle is waiting. There the plastic framed portrait of our little graduate continues to smile serenely.

As I look back at the departing families I think how blessed they are. Life, for them, remains safe. They do not even have to be aware of how lucky they are.

We have always been a family of celebrations. Graduations, birthdays and holidays are times for the family to just be together and celebrate each other. But this will be a year of firsts. With each ritual it will be the first time without Michelle.

Many family dinners have been held at the long, white table in our sun room. Michelle always sat at the far end of the table. She found this to be a convenient location close to the bench. She always thought that I did not realize that this was also a convenient location for discreetly sneaking food to the dog.

Now there is an empty place at that long, white table. On Mother's Day I automatically set a place there. All too quickly my tears reminded me that there will always be an empty place at this table.

I do not even want to think about Christmas this year. It has always been a tradition that every Christmas Eve we all share a candlelight dinner at the long white table. After dinner, without even thinking about it, we slip into our regular seats on the couch and chairs in the living room. The kids have always claimed the central floor space which they share with the dog.

Stan, in his traditional role as Santa, follows his corny routine of ringing the rope of bells that has hung on the mantel since our own children were little. Wearing his Santa hat, he passes out the presents, one by one.

The kids generally provide suggestions as to the order in which the presents are to be opened. Each gift is passed around to be admired before the next gift is passed out.

Michelle, who under her "I am a powerful woman" stance, was always the sweet, sentimental one. Some Christmases she wrote and presented personal poems, that were really odes, to some lucky recipient.

One Christmas when she was still young enough to be in her fort building stage, Michelle presented an ode to Stan in gratitude for all the many afternoons of woodland hikes and fort construction with Brian and Patrick. In those days she was still one of the guys.

THE BEST KIND OF LOVE
by
Michelle Miller

"I'll always follow your way
I'll love you more every day
Having you, Poppy,
You have a heart of gold
It is the best treasure
Which will never get old.
I realize how lucky I am for having you in my life
From all these pictures of this and videos of that
Do you realize
How much you mean to us?
Do you know
How much we all love you?
You have the best kind of love around
It will never fade away."

As a family we keep trying to let go a little more each day. I don't believe that letting go ever means forgetting. It just means cherishing the memories while trying to accept that Michelle is truly gone. I'm still not very good at this.

Like everyone else, Kevin still leaves notes in the mailbox at Michelle's grave. He laments what will never be and shares the kind of paternal love and acceptance that every adolescent would be lucky to have.

> *"Hi Michelle, I'm sitting at your grave writing this, still trying to get my head around the finality of your death. I'll never see you again in this world. Every day I come here and tell you I love you. I miss you. I'm sorry I couldn't protect you.*
>
> *But you'll never answer me. I never thought I'd miss you being angry with me but I do miss you trying to stare me down at the dinner table. I miss making you laugh. I miss when you'd ask me to rub your back and say "do that thing to my spine."*
>
> *I could go on forever cause I miss everything about you, even the things that drove me crazy. We had a lot of disagreements, butted heads a lot, but I hope above all that you understood how much I love you and how much I will always love you.*
>
> –Always, your Dad"

Lately, it is the little unexpected writings of Michelle that brings tears to my eyes. It was a touching moment when Pacita showed me Michelle's college application essay.

"I want to follow in my grandmother's footsteps and become a psychotherapist," she had written. It is heartbreaking that we will never get to see what a really great psychotherapist Michelle might have been. If only she hadn't tried to practice too soon.

The "what might have been" has touched us all. Jima, in the final words of her eulogy, speaks for the loss that we all share:

"Michelle, if you are listening to me now, I want you to know that I love you and I miss you.

Home will not be the same without you. Life will not be the same without you. I want you to know that you did more than you know for me. You welcomed me into your family, your home and your life.

You were supposed to be my maid-of-honor and help me raise my children. But God has better plans for you. He needs you in his army for a greater purpose. You are in his hands now and you are safe.

I know that no matter how many pennies I throw in wishing wells and how many wishes I make on fallen eyelashes – I know that nothing will bring you back. So I wish wherever you are now that you are happy and you are at peace."

thirteen

Shiny Brass Buttons

"The truth will set you free.
But first it will piss you off."
-Gloria Steinem

It already has. It is now approaching a year since Michelle was murdered. The simple truths that emerged last April, when the police discovered her lifeless body, have already been distorted, played with and withheld, in their own caricature of the dance of the seven veils.

The original police reports appear to have been shoved under a winding trail that, to me, looks suspiciously like damage control. The reports, now modified, reflect the Army's view rather than the original assessment, as reported by the Montgomery County Police, who were there first and theoretically, at least, should have jurisdiction over the crime scene.

I have already struggled with forgiveness for those in the Army, who knew that the Sergeant was a predator and yet opted to look the other way. So he and a few of his fellow recruiters continued to become intimately involved with underage recruits. Rumor has it that this is considered to be one of the perks of being a recruiter. I keep trying to remind myself that, offensive as those facts are, no one ever suspected that one of these unlawful contacts could end in such tragedy.

Finding forgiveness is even harder when you no longer know who or what you are trying to forgive. Any attempt to get past the official platitudes appears to be as fruitful as trying to punch a giant marshmallow.

The task of forgiving the Sergeant who destroyed a young girl, I have long since handed over to God. What I am finding more difficult to deal with is all those men in shiny brass buttons. On the highest level, they are the ones who have supported the unofficial military code, which continues to allow open season on women. This appears to be a practice that spans all the ranks. And the men in brass buttons are the ones who appear to value damage control over truth.

Even as I complete the chapters of "All That Bright Light," which seeks to share the experience of surviving loss and grief, I have become increasingly haunted by the story behind the story, which began the day Michelle's body was discovered.

When the lead police detective informed the family that the Secretary of Defense was already involved, I should have suspected that the Department of Defense was not just responding to the death of one idealistic, young girl who went off into that dark April night to save the life of her recruiting officer, who betrayed her.

It now appears more likely that the Defense Department's major concern was the current public outrage over the rampant sexual abuse of women in the military. Adding the death of a young recruit to the Army's already tarnished image was not going to play well.

The detective who visited our family that morning shared a graphic description of Michelle's body seated on the Sergeant's lap, as she appeared to be whispering in his ear. That image has now been replaced with an out-of-perspective computerized drawing of Michelle sprawled, flat on her back, on the floor. That shift seems a bit odd. Most people do not move around after death. The repositioning of the body does set the stage to implicate that Michelle took her own life. That would be convenient for the Army publicity- wise.

Although Montgomery County has one of the finest police departments in the country, even they appear not to be immune to pressure from the Army. In a later police report, there appears to be no focus on the assault rifle and multiple rounds of ammunition that were originally reported to have been found at the front door of the apartment. Those would not have been image enhancers either. Since access to the police files is still being denied, I have only questions and no answers. I want to believe that this will change. After all, this is America.

I continue to hope that there are still those in the Defense Department who do not consider truth to be a relative thing, which can be doctored and shifted about to become more palatable.

This is a painful thing to consider. We have good friends in the Army. And I still consider the military to be populated with brave men and women who, like Michelle, have said: "I want to serve my country." But the military also has a broken place. And that place sits squarely in the laps of some of the commanders, all the way up to the Joint Chiefs of Staff.

Never has this fact been more obvious than it was at a recent Senate hearing when the military leaders were being held accountable for the Pentagon's report of the 26,000 reported cases of sexual abuse in the military.

As the Chiefs of Staff sat at attention, their chests puffed out under their four stars and all those rows of shiny, brass buttons. Stoically, they listened to Army General Martin E. Dempsey blandly announce that, due to the distractions of twelve years of war, he had not always checked to see if his subordinates were dealing seriously enough with the cases of sexual abuse.

Perhaps, if the General is too "distracted" to be aware that a reported 26,000 women have been sexually abused, it may well be time for him to retire. Instead of making that a consideration, he acknowledged, "I'll speak for myself: 'I took my eye off the ball a bit in the commands I had.'" A bit?

Sounds like the same philosophy that allowed the ranking officers of an Army recruiting unit to look the other way when a predator in their own ranks continued to exploit young girls. If anyone had paid attention to the fact that the Sergeant had been under investigation since the previous October, Michelle would be alive today. I want to look those officers in the face and say: "You let this happen."

It has been suggested that perhaps the Sergeant was really being investigated for something else. That would explain the delay in allowing him to remain on the job

That is, if you consider the youth involved as simply collateral damage. But "collateral damage" has a face. We will live with the loss of that face forever. And that is what this book is about.

Maybe the Army recruiting officers looked the other way because a higher ranking officer said "do it." That is how it works in the military. There are no "suggestions." When the commander says "do it," he has just told you that "my buttons are bigger than yours."

I fear that our family may never be given the real answers. Now that I have done all that I can do, I am left to hope that there are still leaders out there who want the military to operate under a higher standard, where honor counts more than shiny, brass buttons.

"Doesn't it make you nervous that you have now irritated the Department of Defense?," asks a friend.

"No," I reply. "They are not interested in me because I have already told my story. Now I have only questions, not answers." And besides, to the military I am not significant. I have no buttons."

fourteen

Hope Is The Thing With Feathers

"Hope is the thing with feathers
That perches in the soul—
And sings the tune without the words--
And never stops—at all—
And sweetest—in the Gale—is heard
and sore must be the storm—
That could abash that little Bird
That kept so many warm—
I've heard it in the chillest lands—
And on the strangest sea—
Yet, never, in Eternity,
It asked a crumb—of me."

—Emily Dickinson

All That Bright Light has been my crumb. In the beginning, walking through an overload of grief, I could only take an evening at a time, crying at the computer as I struggled to write Michelle's story.

But writing this story is the closest I can come to providing some semblance of "fairness" for Michelle. And fairness was always important to her. It seems like only yesterday that I kept receiving those evening calls from that sweet little girl.

"Allie, I'm not being treated fairly," a soft, unhappy little voice would inform me. Then came the litany of wrongs that had befallen her. In those kinder days, the reported injustice was usually the tyranny of a too early bedtime or a limit on the pieces of chocolate she had been allowed.

But that final injustice that life dealt her, I did not get to hear – not in time. Instead, I have only been able to tell her story. And it makes me smile to imagine that I can hear our Lulu saying, "Way to go, Allie!"

It is too late for our beloved Michelle, but if even one person reads this book and hears what can happen and thus, someone else's beloved child is saved, then it will have been worth all the tears.

That is my hope: that, after reading this story, one kid thinks twice before enlisting while they are still in high school; or thinks twice before she races out into the night to save a depressed person with a gun; or one young girl meets an older man who dazzles her, but thinks twice before trusting him. Then this book will have served its purpose.

For us, it has been ongoing support of family, friends and the church, which has helped us to keep our own hearts open through the grief. It was just this past Sunday that Roy Howard, my own pastor, once again, did what he does so well – hit me right where I live. I can only do justice to his words by repeating them:

> *"Something happened to the baptismal bowl. It occurred sometime on Christmas Eve with the hot glow of candlelight underneath its rim. When the tiny crack on the glass was first pointed out to me I was upset, not angry, just disappointed that the beauty of the bowl was now marred. Forever.*
>
> *Then something different occurred to me.*
>
> *I think a symbol of the Church fulfills its purpose best when it actually connects to what is real. And what is more real than the fact that we are not perfect people? Yes, you are God's beloved, but you are also a person who is... ...how shall I put it?......slightly cracked. It may be so slight that you hardly*

notice and probably others don't notice about you. On the other hand some of us have cracks that are obvious to anyone who spends even a passing moment with us. Let's just say my family is well aware that I am cracked. And, sorry to put it this way: so are you.

Augustine thought the cracks come with the human condition and are embedded in being mortal. He echoes what Saint Paul says so honestly about his struggles to be faithful: 'I do not understand my own actions… …The good that I wish to do, I don't do and the evil that I do not want to do, is what I do.' Henri Nouwen, of blessed memory, speaks of "The Wounded Healer." 'Our wounds once healed, remain with us; something like the permanent scars that remind you of the time you scraped your knees or broke your heart. From these healed wounds we are capable of joining in empathy with others whose wounds remain places of pain.'"

Pacita, Michelle's mother, was born knowing this. Even in the well of her own grief, she was deeply touched by the newspaper story of another mother who had lost her own child in a tragic accident. Following her heart, Pacita paid a visit to the other grieving mother. The two women wept together as they nurtured each other. Now there is a new friend in her life.

And that is just the way it works. The giver has become the receiver. This reality has been beautifully expressed in the words of the hymn, The Servant Song. The last few lines of that song will always bring tears to my eyes because they speak to our own experience on a painful journey which has been shared by people of faith who have been there for us.

"I will weep when you are weeping
When you laugh, I'll laugh with you
I will share your joy and sorrow
Till we've seen this journey through."

–Richard Gillard

This is the voice of hope.

Sometimes hope springs up where you least expect it. Recently, it came to me in a heartwarming message from a young Army chaplain, who texted to say that even though she was not a big fan of wars, she had joined the Army "because I knew that there is a great need in the military for a spiritual presence and support for the young men and women, who I knew I could never have a chance to connect with if I had stayed within the confines of a parish"

Grace is everywhere, even in the Army.

Sometimes grace just comes up and smacks you in the face. Kevin and Pacita already know this. Every day they return to Michelle's grave, sometimes just to sit in silence with their daughter. Recently, they were surprised to discover an enormous bouquet of deep red roses with a note that began: "I am so sorry, Michelle. My deepest sympathy to you, your family and friends. No words can express my sorrow. Rest peacefully." It soon became clear that this was a gift from the widow of the Sergeant who had killed Michelle.

"What a beautiful spirit she has," we all thought. She must have experienced her own painful time, yet she still had the caring to reach out to our family. After connecting through Facebook, a dinner together followed. And, as we might have expected, although a very different person, this young woman was like Michelle in her warmth and caring. This could not have been easy for her at first. But her generosity of spirit has come as a piece of grace for our family.

It is these young people, plus many of Michelle's friends, who continue to show up, that give us hope and remind us that the good in the world far outweighs the evil. They are our future. And this is where hope begins: the hope that cracks the pain and lets in the light. It is just as the poet, Emily Dickinson would say:

"Hope is the thing with feathers,
That perches in the soul–
And sings the song without the words—
And never stops—at all."

All That Bright Light is nearly completed and it is now time for me to learn a new mantra from the healing words that I have heard from those who have found strength from the wisdom of AA: "Let go and let God."

And that is the thing with feathers that perches in my soul.

fifteen

All That Bright Light

"All that bright light gone from this world."

–Jacqueline Kennedy

"We thought of you with love today,
But that is nothing new.
We thought about you yesterday,
And the days before that too.
We think of you in silence,
We often speak your name,
Now all we have are memories,
And your picture in a frame.
Your memory is our keepsake,
With which we'll never part.
God has you in his keeping,
We have you in our heart.
It broke our heart to lose you,
But you didn't go alone,
For a part of us went with you...
The day God took you home.

–Author unknown

"We have to let her go, Mom," says Pacita as we sit by the grave.

"Yes we do," I agree. And then we both weep. Letting go is just not that easy.

Grief, I have learned, is like a cocoon, which from the beginning has encased me in its pain. Now, gradually I need to learn to emerge from that sorrow if I am ever again to fully embrace life. The hole in my heart may never go away. But time, I believe, will smooth the rough edges. The hole, however, remains.

"It is better to have loved and lost than never to have loved at all," said Shakespeare. I used to find that quote to be quite sanctimonious and annoying. Now, with experience, I know that he was right. I would never be willing to give up the joy of having Michelle in our lives if that was the only way to erase today's pain.

The capacity to love another so deeply is a powerful gift. But it is also a double-edged sword which renders us vulnerable to the pain of losing the beloved. Once again I am reminded that this precious life is so short and whatever matters most should be attended to now.

"What can I do to help?" my friends still ask. Just being there is what they can do. Hugs help, too. It's really all they can do. Sometimes I find myself replying:

"When you get home be sure to hug your kids."

Although Stan and I no longer have Michelle to hug, we have used the garden to help soothe our sorrow. Within our large garden we have created a small memory garden for Michelle. The yellow roses and flowering lantana call to the butterflies. And white azaleas and ferns surround the large Kousa dogwoods.

Sheltered amid the dogwoods is the life-size stone angel, who gracefully reminds us of our own wild angel whose free spirit has now moved on. Like our own high spirited Michelle, this serene angel, with wings spread for flight, also sports her own dog tags and camouflage hat. Michelle in death – as in life – is an angel with attitude.

As I sit on the old stone bench facing our angel, I smile. And sometimes I just weep for our once and always "Little Lulu." Her precious life was cut short in the midst of bloom that was yet to come to full flower.

Michelle's friends, they know this. Now they come to the garden to stand by the stone trough which holds her memory rocks. The potato-size rocks are round and solid reflecting their own lengthy passage in time. Better known as river jack, these stones, through time and the elements, have become faded and smooth.

It is on these worn rocks that the kids write their goodbyes. Solemnly, they add their own messages to the growing pile. Their words remain, eloquently speaking of the bright light that is forever gone from this world:

> *"Michelle, you honestly are one of the happiest people I know. I looked up to you. And I will never forget our trip to the beach. We are #1 and always will be."*
>
> *"Michelle, you are an inspiration, even now you continue to inspire and pull all of us close together. You are beautiful forever. I know that you are watching over us."*
>
> *"Michelle, I love you and miss you so much! You will always be in my heart. I hope that you will find peace in heaven."*
>
> *"Meesh, I miss you so much. This garden reminds me of you. It's almost as beautiful as you... ...Keep the sun shining. Love you always... ..."*
>
> *"Little sister—I miss you, your smile, your laugh, your beautiful face. It is not the same here without you. I will never forget the times we shared... ..."*
>
> *"Meesh, Thanks for being the best #1 I could ever look up to."*
>
> *"#1 Michelle, There are really no words to describe how much everyone misses you. Although we only had a short time together, you taught me so much. Your carefree and positive attitude always brightened the room. I will carry on both of*

those attitudes every day from now on. Keep an eye on your girls and we will always keep you close to our hearts."

"Meesh, I can't even begin to describe how much I miss you and want to see that beautiful white smile of yours... ...This garden is so absolutely beautiful, just like you. You are the only person I would have trusted to take ——to the prom. I'll see your beautiful face and smile again soon. Rest peacefully in paradise."

"Michelle, how does a person say goodbye to someone like you? You've honestly been such a role model! During soccer last year I wanted to be as good as you. Running with you made a huge difference to my outlook every day."

"It's hard to think that you won't be here playing music at practice, making fun of every coach and just making us laugh. You've made a huge impact on everyone you know. I hope one day I can be as amazing a person as you. I love you so much, Meesh."

"Michelle #1 – I love and miss you so much! You will always be in my heart. I hope that you will find peace in Heaven."

"Michelle, you are lucky to have such an amazing family and friends support system. I have few memories with you but all the ones I have are wonderful. I really did look up to you a lot and I miss you so much. Your laugh and smile are unforgettable. I love you so much and I hope that you are watching over us."

"Meesh, you were such an amazing person and your free spirit has brought joy to so many lives. You were an amazing student, athlete and friend. You have changed my life and taught me so much and I will cherish all these things forever."

"You were a true angel from Heaven. You will be remembered forever. #1 on the field and #1 in our hearts. I love you."

Although your voice is forever stilled, Michelle, the stones, they know and they will speak for you. They tell of a young life that was blessed with the love of family and friends.

If your stone angel had a plaque on it, I would carve the words that the poet, Raymond Carver wrote and had inscribed on his own tombstone. They could have been written for you:

"And did you get what
you wanted from this life, even so?
I did.
And what did you want?
To call myself beloved and to feel myself
Beloved on this earth."

So Michelle, once again here I sit on this little stone bench and watch the butterflies flitting through the lantana and the birds fighting over who gets the next turn in the birdbath.

In the background is the old stone trough filled with the words of love from your friends. And I know that Pacita is right. We need to let you go. You are now in God's hands.

As the warm sun filters through the Kousa dogwood leaves, the garden gently reminds me that the sun will continue to shine again. Even with the hole in that part of my heart that will always belong to Michelle.

Goodbye, our precious Little Lulu. Your bright light may be gone from this world but I know that it will shine through into the next.

sixteen

The Heart Behind The Stone

"To everything there is a season and a time
to every purpose under heaven:

A time to be born and a time to die; a time to plant
and a time to pluck up that which is planted;

A time to kill and a time to heal; a time to
break down and a time to build up;

A time to weep and a time to laugh; a time
to mourn and a time to dance;

A time to cast away stones and a time to gather stones together;
a time to embrace and a time to refrain from embracing;

A time to get and a time to lose; a time to
keep and a time to cast away;

A time to rend and a time to sew; a time to
keep silence and a time to speak;

A time to love and a time to hate; a time of war and a time of peace.

–Ecclesiastes 3: 1-8

As we approach the second anniversary of Michelle's death, the way we grieve takes on a different shape for each of us.

"I live like I don't have tomorrow now," Patrick told a Gazette reporter at last year's gravesite memorial for Michelle.

Although the floodgates of tears have spilled over many times in our family, Patrick, who feels the pain no less, is not a weeper. He remains the "strong, silent one."

In our culture being a strong man is so overrated. And it can lead to the risk of becoming what Thoreau called one of the many men who lead "lives of quiet desperation." How painful for Patrick, who was always the loving, protective big brother, to know that, this one last time, he could not protect his little sister. No one could.

"It would be a lie," Patrick told the reporter, "to say that things were getting easier, that it actually felt like a year had passed since she died. It's like re-living it. It's like it happened yesterday. It actually feels impossible."

That, sadly, is the nature of grief. In the beginning the pain is so overwhelming it seems unbearable. But, with time and support, the survivors learn to hold the loved one in their heart and ultimately move on to rediscover a full and meaningful life.

There is no timetable for this process. Any professional, no matter how well meaning, who tries to walk the survivor through the steps of grieving, as if those steps were an absolute process; has obviously never been there themself.

Instead, we have learned to accept each other's attempts to cope. All too well, we know that you have to give the heart time to accept what the head already knows. She is not coming back.

In this digital era there is always the siren song of the ever present I-pad, jammed with all the photos of those happy days with our loved one. Almost like a dream, for a few brief moments, we escape that terrible reality. But there is a price to be paid for this. I can only struggle to describe this in a poem:

A DIGITAL GRIEF

It was every family's worst nightmare that week,
when every newspaper and television broadcast
featured the brutal death of Michelle.
our beloved child.

Finally, when the media vans were gone,
signaling that Michelle had now become
yesterday's news,
we struggled through the funeral
and all the rituals of death.

And only then did that cold reality sink in.
Michelle was dead.
She was never coming back.
All that remained was that empty, numbing grief.

I wonder, was grieving the death of a beloved child
easier in earlier years,
when the visual memories would only have been captured
on old photographs?

In time, those images would have begun to dim
as that crisp, shiny photographic paper
became brittle with age.
Then, for the survivors,
the healing would gently begin.
With time, old friendships might once again be welcomed.
. Gradually, the clouds would part
and let some light come shining through.

So, I wonder, is the sorrowing easier or harder today
with the advent of digital grief?
The ever-present I-pad,
whose pictures never dim with time
keeps the images of our lost love always present.

With the click of a finger,
there she is, our beloved Michelle.
Look! She lives on!
Joyous…laughing…singing…dancing.
Just like before…
right there in front of us.
In that brief moment we need no one else
for there is our dear Michelle……..
Until we try to tough that beloved face
and our fingers feel only
the cold, transparent glass.
Yet, over and over again,
Like a moth to the flame, we return
a hundred times a day.
So that, for just one more time,
our Michelle will come alive.
Laughing back into our lives.
And a hundred times a day
She dies all over again.

U.S. ARMY

Remaining in that painful place is not an option. Fortunately, we have all been blessed with a lot of help from our friends, who have gathered with us for the good times that serve to remind us that life can also be filled with fun and joy.

Michelle's friends continue to lift the family's spirits with repeated visits and notes. Kevin and Pacita keep up with most of the high school games to watch "their girls," who still remain on the teams. There is no longer a #1 team jersey on the field. The #1 is now retired.

A cherished trophy for the family is the plaque that was presented for Michelle:

Rockville High School
Girls Soccer
Unsung Hero
Michelle Miller

The plaque was for athletic prowess on the field. The "Unsung Hero" was for the heart that she brought to it.

Michelle's many friends will probably never know what comfort they have brought to the family with all their stories and memories. Lauren Marple shared an essay that spoke eloquently of the power of a friendship that transcends death:

Keeping Her Spirit Alive.....

"The silence that fell over the football field of Rockville High School was almost tangible, as nearly a thousand people turned their tear-streaked faces up toward the sunset......

It was the perfect vigil to honor you. We cleared out the shelves of Party City, taking every color of balloon imaginable. Each balloon was special and different, some with a simple Sharpie heart drawn on and some with full-length essays scribbled out, emptying the contents of our hurting hearts onto the latex globe.

We gathered on the field that you dominated with the number one on your back, and released the balloons all at once. It was colorful and carefree and it captured your spirit beautifully.

Along with the balloon strings, we let go of our hurt and pain. I wouldn't consider myself a devoutly religious person, but for me, surrendering my bundle of balloons to the breeze was a physical way of giving up my heavy heart to God.

A week before the start of ninth grade, my dad had a bad accident that landed him in the hospital with a morphine button, as well as casts and scars to spare. I hardly knew you then, but you came running up to me at school and pulled me in for a hug, telling me that you were there for me if I needed it. For the next few weeks, you continued to check up on me and kept reminding me to "hang in there, bud."

You were that person for a lot of people, the person that checked up on others to see how they were doing. You were remarkably intuitive and had a gift for relating to people.

If someone wasn't okay and was struggling with something in their life, you made a point of doing your best to help out in any way possible. Sometimes just the asking and the effort was enough. As an aspiring psychotherapist for veterans, with a particular soft spot in your heart for the Wounded Warriors Project, you cared deeply about those around you.

After that tragic Monday in April, there were mere weeks left of everyone's time together as seniors. We began the slow realization that life is short. Many of us would part ways after crossing that stage in our caps and gowns.

We also began to realize that, like those cute stick figure shirts say, life is good. We began to appreciate one another. We began to have pride in our school and in our classmates. We stopped taking life, and each other for granted. We referred to *ourselves as a community, as a family. As you had done for so many of us in the past, we reached out to one another, offering our support in whatever ways we could give it.........*

I think that we should take our cue from her and strive to be the best people all-around, wherever our lives may take us. Learning to live without someone is a terrible thing, but learning to live with them in your heart can be wonderful............

The age-old question we all found ourselves asking was "why do the good die young?" It's not fair. A wife who loses her husband is called a widow. A child who loses his or her parents is called an orphan. There is no word, however, for a parent who loses a child, or for a person who loses a friend.

The pain is indescribable. There's never a good answer as to why someone is taken from us, and it's never, by any means a good feeling, but good can come out of it. I think that instead of wondering why the good die young, we should ask what we can do to let the good continue to live.

Since Michelle's death, I've done my best to keep her spirit alive by striving to be the same kind of person that she always was. I don't think that the world will ever have the answer to the question, and that's okay. Life goes on somehow and so does the good if we let it."

Lauren Marple

How right she is.

I still continue to hear the heartwarming stories of people whose lives Michelle touched with little acts of kindness that she never even felt the need to mention.

At a recent book signing for All That Bright Light, I propped up a large poster of Michelle proudly wearing her camouflage, a small innocent smile and looking even younger than her 17 years. Lettered over her photograph were the words: "Collateral Damage Has a Face."

During a lull between the groups of onlookers I became aware that one young man remained. Silent and motionless, he continued to stare at Michelle's photograph. Handsome and tall, the young man, a boy really, had the eyes of someone who has known their own sadness. I touched his arm.

"You knew her, didn't you?"

The young man nodded. Then, hesitantly, he recounted his experience the previous year when he was a senior transfer student at Michelle's high school. Knowing no one, he sat alone in the cafeteria. Anyone who has ever been a high school student knows the hierarchy of the lunchroom.

Who sits where and with whom can be a spirit-breaking experience if you are not one of the kids at the "popular" table or, at the very least, with your own circle of friends.

But, recalled my young friend, smiling sadly, he was not alone for long. His solitude was soon interrupted by the appearance of a beautiful, young girl, our Michelle. Having no need to prove herself at the "popular" table, she just followed her heart.

"Hi! You're new here, aren't you?" Michelle smiled as she joined him. "I'll introduce you," she offered and then stayed to listen to his story. This was not Michelle just being polite. This was Michelle really wanting to know him. He knew that. And so, he was no longer alone.

Soon after that, Michelle's gravestone was erected over that slight mound of earth amid the new shoots of grass and the many flowers and memorials that continued to arrive from those who loved her. At first, looking at that massive stone was almost too painful to bear. It had become just one more reality check. Our Michelle was really gone forever.

The new gravestone is shaped like a large heart, not the traditional stone that I would have preferred. I wanted a heavy, old stone carved with a cross, solid and enduring. Pacita wanted the big heart. So I kept my mouth shut. This is her baby and Pacita will be here day after day.

But now I look at that large heart and I think what could be more fitting? Like the stone that honors her, Michelle's legacy is not her honor roll status or her athletic prowess. It is her great big heart that has touched so many.

And like those others before him, that one lonely young man will probably hold her forever in his heart.

As do we.

seventeen

Not Here. Present Elsewhere

"If I can stop one heart from breaking,
I shall not live in vain;
If I can ease one life the aching,
Or cool one pain,
Or help one fainting robin
Unto his nest again,
I shall not live in vain."
–Emily Dickinson

Michelle is stardust now. I find it comforting when a Quaker friend reminds me, that in the Aramaic Bible the words for death translate as, "Not here. Present elsewhere."

The message behind those comforting words was eloquently expressed in a poem written by a friend of Michelle's, who obviously felt profound respect for her. After Michelle's tragic death, the young poet, who chose to remain anonymous, but also wished to have his words be heard, submitted "Eulogy for Michelle" to a high school literary publication.

Eulogy for Michelle

Hindsight beckons through her angelic mind,
In heaven, she has earned omniscience.
Behind the body mourned on earth
Lies a life dedicated to the salvation of others,
A soul celebrated by the omnipotent.

She takes the same path she took on Earth.
It is not a decision of death that drives her,
But a focus on the life in need.
Understanding the risk does not stop her.
This is courage.

It is the path of the righteous to consider others.
He was sinking,
Desperately clawing at the crashing nothingness.
Her torch was far-reaching,
But the vast darkness was overwhelming.

Yet her smile still shines in the afterlife.
She drowned as she had lived.
Nobly, head held high,
Knowing she did the right thing.
One day this will be clear to all.

–Anonymous

So it is for the community of faith. We believe that we are all spiritual beings. Upon death, we are gone from this earth.

Now we have moved elsewhere. The grieving that follows belongs to those who remain.

For the survivors, an old Hasidic saying promises: "God's love is placed on our hearts so that when they are broken open by the pain of life, that love will fall into the open seam of pain."

In our own family, that love has been manifested in the support of all the caring people who have been there for us. I am now choosing to let this love soak in, rather than putting any more psychic energy into the Army. Instead, I choose to remember the young Lieutenant at Fort Mead, who handed me Michelle's dog tags and solemnly reminded me that "We are not all like that." I believe him.

Michelle certainly would have believed him. She died, still dreaming in her fierce, little heart that one day she would be there to help the wounded warriors. Instead, she became one.

"If only….." is a trap that we are all learning to go beyond. It is time to accept that we were indeed blessed to have shared those 17 years with Michelle. But sometimes we slip. It still makes me teary when I recall that touching moment when I read the words that Michelle wrote in her college applications: "I want to follow in my grandmother's footsteps and become a psychotherapist."

"If only" I had become a dog trainer or an accountant instead, I agonized. But it would have made no difference, I now realize. For Michelle was always in the business of helping others.

Sadly enough, when she confronted evil, Michelle did not recognize it. More than once, my Quaker friend has gently suggested that I let go of this "if only" thinking.

"Michelle put her life on the line for what she believed," he reminds me.

"Don't try to re-write that."

I am not going to re-write anything. Instead, I believe that Michelle's life can be summed up by another, more famous author:

The purpose of life is not to be happy.
It is to be useful,
to be honorable,
to be compassionate,
to have it make some difference that
you have lived and lived well."

–Ralph Waldo Emerson

And that she did.

The part of living well that Emerson does not dwell on, is the ability to be happy and joyous. Michelle had that part down pat. Remembering that part and how fully she lived those 17 years helps with the grief. There are so many memories to embrace.

Sometimes those memories are just the simple, little things that we always took for granted. Now, when we share another family dinner at Clyde's I can finally enjoy dessert again, smiling at the memories of sitting with Michelle and laughing over who ate the most of the crème brulee that we always shared together.

I will never forget our funny, fierce little girl, winning on the athletic field, laughing and carousing with her friends –and just taking in life with a gigantic gulp. Michelle's enthusiasm was contagious and she could always be assured that someone would participate in the latest fun idea that she had cooked up. I was certainly not immune to that enthusiasm one afternoon when we went to the mall after Michelle had tactfully informed me that I needed to be aware that I would be the absolute antithesis of cool if I continued to wear wide-legged slacks.

By the end of the day I had been dragged into several of the stores that I would normally have rapidly walked past. Instead, this time I emerged with several pairs of painted-on, skintight pants with 2- inch zippers and no breathing room, which were promptly dubbed my "slut pants." I still smile every time I wear them.

I smile a lot more now. The transforming power of love in our lives continues to guide us to a new day. Patrick is now taking IT courses and relaxes on the basketball court with his friends. The beautiful, ever-present Jima is now studying psychology and shines as a major force in Patrick's life. One day, we hope, she will become his bride and the beloved daughter and granddaughter in our family.

It is, indeed, a new day. Kevin and Pacita have now turned lonely weekends into jaunts to the Chesapeake Bay and West Virginia. Kevin has been so deeply touched by the ongoing support of Saint Mary's Catholic church, which is Pacita's church, that he now wants to make it his own. Already, he attends weekly (RCIA) Rite of Christian Initiation of Adult classes in anticipation of the day that he, too, becomes a Catholic.

Recently, Pacita and Kevin celebrated the enduring strength of their relationship with a renewal of their wedding vows. With Patrick and Jima as witness attendants, they formally wed in the beautiful old chapel of Saint Mary's, their source of so much love and caring.

As the healing continues the good time memories of our beautiful, exuberant child come flooding through.

She embraced life with such passion. We smile now remembering Michelle's early adolescence when she adored the singer, Jesse McCartney, with all her young heart.

"I am going to marry him," she frequently announced. Her future "game plan" was even adjusted so that her career could accommodate her marriage to Jesse, whose giant poster adorned her bedroom wall.

"You and your beautiful soul...," the words to one of McCartney's most famous songs, became Michelle's theme. She and a friend spent one delightful afternoon alone in the house with the music cranked up full volume as together they raced through the house belting out the lyrics, "You and your beautiful soul" at the top of their lungs. Even at the end of Michelle's life "Beautiful Soul" remained her theme.

Michelle, you are stardust now. We are left with the memories of our beautiful, passionate girl and with the knowledge that you will always live on in the hearts of all those many who loved you—you and your beautiful soul.

adidas
MILLER
1

Epilogue

A Final Truth

Since the day the broken body of my 17-year-old granddaughter, Michelle, was discovered in the apartment of her 31-year-old Army recruiting sergeant, the facts surrounding her death have been distorted or withheld. The police detective who notified our family stated that Michelle had been shot and murdered by the sergeant, who then used his gun to kill himself.

The detective assured us that justice would be done, and that this case was so important that the Secretary of Defense had already been notified. All too soon, we realized that this notification had little to do with justice; it was all about damage control. What followed was a blackout of facts, while the Army "investigated."

Their investigation involved a shell game of changing theories as to the manner of Michelle's death, some actually insinuating that she had committed suicide (all evidence to the contrary). After three years of delay, an attorney has finally received the Army's report – and it is damning.

I once thought that I could take on the Department of Defense and set the record straight. Michelle's memory deserves to be honored, and it is time for the truth to come out. This is my swan song.

Copies of Michelle's story, *All That Bright Light,* have been mailed with this epilogue to selected members of Congress and the Senate and investigative reporters. Now it is in their hands. If the Department of Defense attempts to quash the truth and wins, then we all lose.

Those especially vulnerable are the young recruits who are the future of tomorrow's military. As Michelle's father, Kevin Miller, pointed out: "The Army has such a stellar record for dealing with sexual abuse within its ranks: ignoring and covering up." However, he added, "I have nothing but respect for our fine military men and women, but the brass needs to come down hard on the outliers who ruin, and in some cases, end lives."

I, too, wish to express my respect and acknowledge the enormous debt of gratitude our country owes to the brave men and women of the military who have dedicated their lives in service to their country. Too many have died and too many have been broken in body and spirit. Those are the wounded warriors to whom we owe so much. With their actions they have said, "I want to serve my country."

These were Michelle's exact words as a high school honor student, when she fell for the siren song of an Army recruiter. In one of our last videos of Michelle, she is proudly wearing her new camo fatigues, belting out the Army song. The song's last refrain "and the Army goes rolling along" proved to be prophetic, for that is exactly what the Army did – they rolled right over her. This is why I am compelled to share the truth about the tragic end of Michelle's young life.

As an honors student, a charismatic Army recruiter's promise of a college scholarship was Michelle's enticement to enlist in the Army while still in high school. Days after her death, a form letter from the Army arrived in the mail addressed to Michelle. The letter stated that her college scholarship had been rescinded due to budget cuts. This was the least of the damages inflicted upon her.

Although just a recruit who never lived to see a day of service, Michelle, too, was a wounded warrior. She followed the Army code of never leaving a wounded comrade. So, that April night when her recruiting sergeant sent yet another of many texts begging her to come because he was feeling suicidal, Michelle went off into that dark night to save him. But she never returned.

It is only now, after three years, that the Army has acknowledged the fact that the comrade was the sergeant, who began to seduce Michelle from the day he recruited her. All along, the Army knew about the sergeant's history of alcohol and substance abuse, multiple suicide attempts, and past inappropriate conduct with multiple recruits, some still minors. Apparently, these were not sufficient reasons to remove a recruiter who was so successful at signing up young future soldiers.

What has finally emerged is that prior to Michelle's death, on at least two separate occasions, two fellow sergeants had intervened at the request of a third party and assisted with the removal of multiple loaded firearms from the recruiter's residence, because there was a reported fear that he would harm himself or others. After these incidents, the sergeants returned his firearms to him and failed to notify their chain of command that loaded weapons were in the home of a known suicidal and potentially violent soldier. There later proved to be multiple others who were aware not only of this, but also of the fact that the recruiting sergeant was continuing an unauthorized relationship with Michelle which put her in grave danger.

A few nights prior to Michelle's death, the sergeant was informed by one of his higher-ranking friends that he was to be reported to headquarters the coming Monday morning, thus effectively signing Michelle's death warrant for that Sunday night. On Saturday, the sergeant had texted another recruiter with the query: "Where can I hide a dead body?"

How, I wonder, do these men live with themselves? And how can the Army justify hiding these facts, as well as distorting the reality of the way in which Michelle died?

We didn't know that it could get any worse until we read the Post Mortem Examination of the Chief Medical Examiner for the State of Maryland. The blood spatter pattern analysis had already established that Michelle had died first. But it did not prepare us for the violence she must have experienced before death.

There were additional injuries to her head, torso, and upper and lower extremities. The bullet entered the right side of her head at the temple. The wound path was directed right to left and slightly upward, with no front/back direction and massive destruction in the frontal portion of her brain.

An additional disturbing fact was that in the neck (at a significant distance from the bullet trajectory at her temple) the C1/C2 cervical spinal column joint was fracture dislocated (widely separated) with soft tissue hemorrhage within the joint space. The hemorrhage indicates that Michelle was alive at the time her neck was fractured. From that moment on, she would have been paralyzed, unable to move or defend herself in the period prior to the bullet entering her brain. We can only guess what she may have endured.

The pain and stress of re-living the terrible way that Michelle died has become too debilitating for me to continue trying to be heard. It is my hope that the people who have received copies of *All That Bright Light,* will press for Congress to finally pass a bill that would require sexual assault and felony murder within the military be tried in civilian courts, where justice might prevail. A good beginning would be for Congress to also mandate that military recruiters be kept out of high schools, where there is too much opportunity to prey on the young and vulnerable.

As for me – no more. I have done what I can. Sometimes in life you just have to do your best and then let go and offer it up.

I find myself identifying with Chief Joseph of the Nez Perce, who with his people tried to prevent the government takeover of their land. Ultimately, he surrendered with the parting words: "…I am tired; my heart is sick and sad. From where the sun now stands I will fight no more forever."

Nor will I.